Invitation
to
MAPPER
(I)

Invitation to MAPPER™ (I)

A Pragmatic Approach to End-User Computing and Report Preparation

Harry Katzan, Jr.

a petrocelli book
new york / princeton

Designed by Diane L. Backes
Typesetting by Backes Graphics

Printed in the United States of America
1 2 3 4 5 6 7 8 9 10

Library of Congress Cataloging in Publication Data

Katzan, Harry.
   Invitation to MAPPER.

   Bibliography: p.
   Includes index.
   1. MAPPER (Computer system) I. Title.
QA76.6.K363   1983   001.64'25   83-17222
ISBN 0-89433-222-8

MAPPER™ is a trademark of Sperry Corporation.

Contents

Preface   ix

CHAPTER ONE
A Basis for End-User Computing   1

Introduction   2
The End-User Concept   2
Benefits of End-User Computing   4
Productivity Considerations   4
Operational Environment   5
Management Support   6
Information Systems   8
The 80–20 Rule   9
Evolutionary Systems   10
The Control Point   12
Management's Viable Alternative   14
Organizational Dynamics   14
Escalation of Requirements   16
Summary   17

CHAPTER TWO
MAPPER Fundamentals   21

Introduction   21
MAPPER Database Structure   23
Mode Pairs   24
Report Identification   24
Report Definition   25
Report Creation   26
Line Size   26
Characteristics of a Type   27
Free-Form Lines   27
Types of Lines in MAPPER   27
Report Structure   29

Line Hierarchy   30
Control Line   30
Sign On and the MAPPER Logo   33
Sign Off   35
Summary   35

CHAPTER THREE
Access and Modification Functions   39

Introduction   39
Service Functions   40
Operational Philosophy of MAPPER   44
Line-Oriented Functions   45
Report-Oriented Functions   54
Summary   62

CHAPTER FOUR
Inquiry and Update Functions   65

Introduction   65
The Find Function   69
The Search Function   70
The Locate Function   73
The Sort Function   75
The Binary Find Function   78
The Match Function   80
Overview of Other Manual Functions   82
Summary   83

CHAPTER FIVE
MAPPER Calculations   85

Calculator Facility   85
Totalize Function Overview   88
Horizontal Movement   90
Horizontal Arithmetic   91
Vertical Summation   93

Subtotaling   95
Averaging   96
Overview of Other Totalize Function Operations   98
Summary   99

CHAPTER SIX
MAPPER Run Facility   101

The Run Concept   101
Run Control Line   102
Run Control Statement Format   107
Octal Type Algorithms   109
Variables and Reserved Words   110
Temporary RIDs   112
Utility Runs   113
Run Design   114
Run Control Statements   118
Summary   123

CHAPTER SEVEN
Organizational Dynamics   127

Application Domain   127
The MAPPER Coordinator   130
Information Center Concept   132
Analysis   134

References   137

Index   139

Preface

The unresolved applications backlog in the computer field is in the news these days, and it has called the computer industry's attention to a variety of nonprocedural languages and software facilities, collectively referred to as "end-user systems." The MAPPER system is a principal product in this category. The key objective of these systems is to provide fast access to informational resources and the widespread use of data manipulation facilities on a demand basis.

Informally, the end-user concept refers to the nontrivial use of computer facilities by non-DP personnel. More specifically, the end-user concept refers to three related items:

- End-user systems and languages.
- End-user application development.
- End-user open access to computer facilities.

Thus, the concept effectively puts the power of the computer into the hands of the people who will actually benefit from the increased timeliness of information and the increased productivity—that is, the end-user. An end-user system is neither demand computing nor transaction processing; it is a combination of computer hardware, software, and data communications facilities that provides the functional capabilities of performing traditional DP/MIS operations locally without necessarily having to utilize the services of the data processing department. The primary advantage of end-user computing is economic, and it eventually shows up on the proverbial bottom line.

In an end-user system, data is extracted and summarized from conventional data processing systems, from transaction processing systems, and from external sources. It is stored as application or subject databases. Once data is prepared for an end-user group, it is essentially owned by them. Applications software is prepared by end-user personnel and executed by end-user personnel. The end result is an enterprise-wide set of end-user developed applications that are local to a particular business process or department, when appropriate, and span business and organizational boundaries when necessary. This kind of result is achievable only through computers, but is effective because of the benefits inherent in end-user computing.

There is a growing awareness in the DP/MIS field that data structures and programming languages, as distinct disciplines, can never be totally separated. Moreover, the gradual evolution to end-user computing emphasizes the fact that in many cases, it is preferable to "show" the computer rather than to "tell" it what to do. This practice is sometimes referred to as *visual programming*. The MAPPER system provides a visual programming environment through a user-friendly report-oriented interface. The basic data structure in MAPPER is the report, which permits the end-user to deal in concrete terms with well-defined physical entities rather than abstract logical concepts. The basis for visual programming is well-established in the word processing community.

As a visually-oriented report processing system, MAPPER is unique. Its origins lie in the manufacturing area and not in data processing, and this fact is perhaps evident from its "down to earth" structure and user friendliness. The MAPPER system is a user-driven facility, and many persons feel as though it could never have achieved a correspondingly high level of success if its development had been initiated by software specialists.

The name MAPPER stands for MAintaining, Preparing, and Producing Executive Reports. Literally speaking, it is not a programming language, even though it possesses a well defined user interface. MAPPER is a total report processing system that incorporates the following elements:

- A report oriented database.

- A set of manual user functions for performing data processing, data manipulation operations, for updating, and for reporting.

- A run facility for creating operational lists of MAPPER functions—similar to a macro or subroutine facility.

- A coordinator position, supported by appropriate software and procedures, that involves the general control of the MAPPER system as it relates to the design, development, and use of a report-structured data base.

Drawn from either the user domain or the data processing shop, the coordinator plays a key role by interfacing with DP management, user management, DP personnel, and user personnel.

This book gives an introduction to the MAPPER system and is primarily intended for persons who will design systems and applications. The book can also be used profitably by persons who need background information on end-user systems and nonprocedural languages.

The underlying objective of this book is to promote understanding of the MAPPER concept. With this objective clearly in mind, the subject matter is presented through easy-to-read textual material liberally interspersed with examples. No particular background in either computers or programming is needed to completely understand the book and to learn the MAPPER system. The MAPPER system is an extensive facility, and this book is being offered only as an invitation to a productive future. The MAPPER user's guide should serve as a definitive reference for the design and construction of actual applications.

It is a pleasure to acknowledge the cooperation and assistance of several people: Jorg Heinke, James Mulholland, and Lou Schlueter for information on the MAPPER system; O.R. Petrocelli, the publisher, for the foresight and courage to publish a book on the groundbreaking subject of the MAPPER system; and to my wife, Margaret, for handling the word processing aspects of the job, and for being a good partner during the entire project.

Harry Katzan, Jr.
Millstone Township, New Jersey

CHAPTER ONE

A Basis for End-User Computing

Most organizations are so heavily dependent upon computers that it would be nearly impossible to sustain their everyday activities without them. Clearly, it would be impossible to return to the days of Charles Dickens, when clerks labored for long hours in primitive conditions. Even though computers, data processing, and informational services differ between organizations, most people agree that they achieve their intended purpose through various forms of cost reduction, cost avoidance, and the capability of performing tasks that would otherwise be impossible. This dependence has serious drawbacks, as well as advantages. As organizations evolve to provide better products and services, the various forms of computer support must change as well. In addition, computer hardware prices have been reduced markedly in recent years through advanced design concepts and modern methods of fabrication. These price reductions, however, have not been directly transferable to the organization. The reason is rather well known these days; it amounts to the simple fact that pertinent software is not available to the extent that it is needed, and the situation for both computer support and hardware utilization is not likely to improve. The computer industry reports that there is a shortage of programmers, and this shortcoming is predicted as seriously affecting ongoing applications and future developments. One means of providing support to sustain the momentum of the computer industry is through end-user systems that allow applications to be developed without programmers. This book covers the MAPPER system, which is one of the principal software products in this category. This chapter provides a basis for end-user computing.

Introduction

The potentially disastrous long range effects of the unresolved applications backlog is in the news these days. Fueled by decreasing hardware costs and an increased end-user awareness, this apparent backlog situation has resulted in a "bubbling out" of a variety of nonprocedural languages and systems aimed at putting the power of the computer in the hands of the end-user.

Clearly, the situation is different from that of the increasingly popular world of personal business computers, because the order of the day typically involves concurrent access to a common data base by several persons. While the operational environment may be relatively new, the application needs are traditional among executives, managers, administrators, and other knowledgeable workers. Decision makers have an insatiable appetite for information, and it is invariably needed "yesterday." Thus, the key objective continues to be faster access to information and the widespread use of data manipulation facilities on a demand basis.

The End-User Concept

The basic idea behind end-user computing is conceptually rather obvious, but it certainly is not simple to implement technically and institute in an organizational environment. In fact, analogous situations have previously existed both in and out of the computer field. In the early days of the telephone industry, for example, when the exciting possibilities of remote communications were just catching on, all calls were routed manually through a telephone operator. The rate of growth of personnel to switch calls was comparable to the growth of subscribers, providing a serious limitation on the expansion of facilities and the level of customer service. (Clearly, a telephone is no more than a novelty if the range of calls that can be made is constrained.) Only through the implementation of automatic switching equipment was the telephone industry able to progress to its current level of function. The key point here is that the end-user of the telephone effectively does his or her own switching through the "dialing" system. Similarly, the early days of the computer field were characterized by a shortage of trained assembler language programmers. After the invention of higher-level languages, such as BASIC, FORTRAN, and COBOL, the industry was effectively opened up, and really able to take off and achieve its present level of success and phenomenal growth. The extensive use of timesharing (also called demand processing) provides yet another example of this obvious but often neglected concept.

In the domain of computer-based information systems, the *End User Concept* refers to three related items:

- *Systems and Languages.* The development and widespread availability of systems and languages that provide easy-to-use facilities for accessing data bases, generating ad hoc reports, and performing a variety of other computational and data processing facilities.

- *Application Development.* The use of end-user facilities, by personnel who are not data processing specialists, to design procedures and perform tasks traditionally done by computer programmers and analysts.

- *Open Access.* The actual execution of computer "processes" on end-user systems by relatively untrained people to generate computer results.

Thus, the end-user concept places the power of the computer into the hands of the people who will eventually benefit from the results that are generated. The key question is clearly not, "Who is pushing the buttons?" but rather, "What is the most expeditious way of getting the job done with the factors of productivity and optimum performance in mind?"

It is also important to realize what is and what isn't an end-user system in the present context. An end-user system, for example, permits an executive, manager, administrator, or one of their designees to prepare a computer-generated report or set of computed results on an unplanned ad hoc basis without going through a computer-trained intermediary. Moreover, the results are ordinarily available through end-user facilities in a relatively short period of time—such as minutes or hours—depending upon the complexity of the particular task. The "unplanned" aspect of end-user computing refers to the data accessed and also to the precise form of the report or the computations required. Clearly, the report could also be provided in several convenient forms, such as color graphics output, text video display, or on the printed page.

An on-line system is not normally regarded as an instance of end-user computing, even though most end-user systems permit the user to interact with the computer via a terminal device and data communications facilities. An on-line system that allows a salesperson to inquire about the status of an order or an inventory level provides planned operational functions and planned results; only the values of the key variables change due to the specific data required from the underlying DP/MIS system. In addition, the procedures and computer programs for accessing an on-line system are customarily prepared by the DP staff or acquired from external sources on a proprietary basis.

To sum up, an end-user system is a combination of computer hardware, software, and data communications facilities that provides the functional capability of performing traditional DP/MIS operations locally without having to utilize the services of the data processing department.

Benefits of End-User Computing

The primary advantage of end-user computing is economic, and it eventually shows up on the proverbial bottom line. As with office automation, the underlying concepts are technological, but the payoff is the enhanced performance of decision makers. Cost justification is cumbersome, because it ultimately amounts to trading hard money against soft and often intangible results. Also, cost justification is not a matter of simply replacing or reducing support people.

The objective of end-user computing is to enhance the decision-making potential of knowledge workers. If an employee's work is done in half the time and there is no additional work to occupy the newly acquired free time, then the cost effectiveness of a readily accessible informational facility is questionable. On the other hand, if the use of end-user computing can shorten the communication cycle, and if this increased efficiency can be reflected in bottom line improvement, then it is feasible to adopt end-user computing as a means of utilizing the informational resources of the organization.

Productivity Considerations

The subject of productivity is a key issue in most organizations these days. This concern ranges from top management performance to individual worker achievement, and touches on practically every form of activity, including the end-user in a computer environment. Many information systems managers now feel that the broad class of computer users are in the best position to improve their own productivity. Clearly, this cannot be done overnight and without the right tools, but it nevertheless represents a direction and a goal at the same time.

It is becoming apparent that the dynamic operational style of the organization often obscures an employee's ability to make personal productivity gains. Through recent advances in hardware and software technology, end-users do not need the same level of DP training as they did in the earlier days of computing. Thus, management has to develop an organizational philosophy that effectively "lets it happen."

Another consideration is that word processing, electronic mail, and other forms of office automation are already in the professional workplace. End-user management wants systems for end-user computing that can be handled by persons already engaged in some form or another of information technology.

Operational Environment

Productivity is normally tied to people and their work. In the computer-related operational environment of the modern organization, workers— be they executives, managers, administrators, professionals, or clerks— are divided into two broad categories: production workers and knowledge workers. Clearly, managers are usually knowledge workers, for example, and clerks are usually production workers. Some lower level managers are closely associated with and effectively control production workers, so they can essentially be classed with production workers; other managers who work primarily with information have the classification of knowledge worker.

Production workers perform structured tasks prepared in advance. Bank tellers and inventory clerks are generally regarded as production workers. Knowledge workers perform unstructured tasks to sustain operations that are not planned in advance and, additionally, tend to be non-repetitive. Most knowledge workers perform tasks that require varying degrees of creativity and analytical ability.

Production workers are divided into transaction-oriented people and support people; hence the term "support worker" commonplace in the area of office automation. Transaction-oriented people use transaction processing information systems, as in banking and airline reservations, and support people enhance the productivity of knowledge workers through the use of office automation systems and end-user computer systems. Thus, support workers characteristically perform unstructured tasks established on an "as needed" basis.

The class of knowledge workers also includes engineers, scientists, project leaders, analysts, and other specialists, in addition to the wide group of executives, managers, administrators, and professionals mentioned above. Workers in this class have one common element: their work pattern. Characteristically, they accept (or receive) input, perform analyses of various forms, and then prepare output that takes the form of person-to-person communications, reports, and various types of electronic media. In many instances, knowledge workers rely heavily on their support counterpart. In an equal number of cases, however, the knowledge worker could personally take advantage of end-user computer facilities of the sort mentioned above, if it were available to him or her.

Most knowledge workers are comfortable with computer-based information systems in this modern computer age, and generally feel that they could do their job better and more quickly through end-user facilities that permit ad hoc reporting and analysis. Within the scope of organizational policies for data control, these persons additionally benefit from a greater degree of control over the information that actually concerns them.

To sum up, end-user computer facilities can supply a well-defined and systematic business approach to decision making and management control. The approach is well-defined because information is structured for end-user needs and controlled by the end-user group. The approach is systematic because the persons who actually benefit from the informational procedure are the ones who are accessing it.

Management Support

The extension of computer equipment to parts of the organization outside of data processing is certainly not a new phenomena. Both knowledge workers and support workers have been using computers and terminals for many years now in the context of Management Information

Systems (MIS) and Office Automation. However, the strategic direction with end-user computing is the marriage of conventional data processing and traditional MIS, producing a synergistic impact that is several times greater than either of the component technologies taken separately.

A *Management Support System* is a computer-based information system that supports executive, management, and administrative activity. This classification essentially incorporates most aspects of decision support systems, reporting systems, office information systems, and data base systems. As such, end-user computing is a modern version of a management support system, because it supports management through local control over data and computational resources.

There are a lot of systems of this type that involve information, computers, reports, planning, forecasting, and so forth. Periodic reports are generated in some cases and special reports are generated in others. Whereas special-purpose computer programs are often prepared to generate the necessary reports and to perform the required analyses, the current trend is to use general reporting software in order to cut down on the lead time required to develop the computer application. However, a software package in itself does not necessarily constitute an end-user computing system, since packages of this type are commonly used by DP departments in a variety of convenient forms.

As suggested above, key elements that determine an end-user system are:

- Who controls the information.
- Who develops the computer applications.
- Who initiates the computer processing.

In this context, therefore, decision support systems, office information systems, data base systems, and report generator systems are not generally classed as end-user systems—even though they do in fact involve end-users.

In an end-user system, data is extracted and summarized from conventional data processing systems, from transaction processing systems, and from external sources, and it is stored as "application" or "subject" databases. Thus, an end-user system is neither a DP nor an MIS system, but rather a composite of the two. Once data is prepared for an end-user group, it is essentially "owned" by them.

Similarly, applications are prepared by end-user personnel and executed by end-user personnel. Clearly, these applications could be developed by DP or MIS people, but they are not because of the productivity considerations previously discussed. An end-user system—software, applications, and data—requires computer resources and close management attention. The end-user system may run on the same computer facilities as a data processing or transaction processing system, but it is viewed conceptually as a separate system. It is not uncommon, however, to witness standalone end-user systems. When data is needed from a central data processing facility, a disk or tape file is written to achieve the data transfer. The interface program used to write a file from the local computer system also performs summarization, extraction, and selection operations on a particular basis.

Information Systems

The problems of end-user systems are not unlike those of traditional information systems. Plagued by development delays, high maintenance costs, long lead times, and overall system ineffectiveness, information systems management and designers, as well, have stressed the need to relate computer-based systems to the integrated set of business processes. Thus, an information system essentially models the enterprise as a dynamic entity.

Overall systems success in this context involves an increase in the productivity of programmers and analysts, a decrease in systems development costs, a high level of timeliness of information, and facilities that are available when needed. Moreover, it is expected that the information resource is more accurate, more complete, more concise, and more relevant than in predecessor systems. Success of this sort is not a small order, but it can be achieved when the following conditions are met:

- Well-defined requirements for the functionality and general structure of information systems and data base structures are demanded by top management in collaboration with DP management before development or enhancement costs are incurred.

- The end-user participates in the definition of the informational requirements of the object system.

- The object system is defined in terms of relevant business functions rather than being based on existing hardware, software, informational, and organizational structures.

- Centralized control exists over the establishment of application and subject data bases, and the end-user participates in the controlling process.

- Adequate justification is required for new applications through the controlling process, and operations are monitored to ensure they fall within operational constraints determined when the application was certified.

- The end-user participates in the development of computer applications and their subsequent use.

The end result is an enterprise-wide set of end-user developed applications that are local to a particular business process or department, when appropriate, and span business and organizational boundaries when necessary. This kind of result is achievable only through computers, but is effective because of the benefits inherent in end-user computing.

The 80–20 Rule

The "80–20 rule" is a means of conceptualizing the manner in which information flows within an organization; the concept applies equally well to other business functions, such as manufacturing and inventory, and to other organizational situations, such as claims processing and various forms of client (or patient) service. Informally, the 80–20 rule suggests that 80 percent of the action involves only 20 percent of the people, or conversely that 20 percent of the people demand 80 percent of the resources.

In information technology, the 80–20 rule stems from the recognition that an organizational unit functions as a pseudo information processor. Information is summarized as it flows upward; it is expanded and detailed as it flows downward; and it is modified and possibly expanded as it flows horizontally. More formally, therefore, the 80–20 rule states that 80 percent of the information used in a department is generated from within that department and only 20 percent comes from external sources. Alternately, 80 percent of the information processed within the department stays within the department and only 20 percent of the information will be transferred outside of the department.

The 80–20 rule is normally employed for the location of informational and computational resources to achieve optimum performance. The underlying philosophy of distributed data processing is that local control over computer resources, coupled with their judicious placement within the organizational structure, will lead to a higher level of operational effectiveness than is possible with large centralized sites. In addition to providing alternatives that are simply not available in a centralized modality, distributed data processing has provided the promise of computer resources that are responsive to the day-to-day needs of operational management. In short, there is a feeling in some management circles that the large centralized computer complex is an unwieldy structure with a tendency for exerting undue influence over varied managerial activities that are specifically within the computer domain.

In reality, however, the expectations associated with distributed data processing have never totally materialized, because local implementation is frequently performed by inexperienced people, due to the shortage of qualified DP personnel. Clearly, local distributed processing cannot match the economy of scale of large mainframes—in terms of hardware, software, informational, and human performance.

One of the major advantages of end-user computing is that it exists as a feasible alternative to distributed data processing, and in many cases will emerge as the preferable option. What the end-user group essentially desires is control over data, applications, and local operations, and not necessarily control over hardware boxes.

Evolutionary Systems

The way that an end-user system proliferates is through what may be referred to as an "evolutionary system." The end-user software is available from a central data processing facility on a demand, time-sharing, or real-time basis. For the purposes of the end-user, the difference in operational modes is not significant. All that is important is that the end-user, as a person, has access to computer facilities through a Video Display Unit (VDU) with a keyboard via data communications facilities. Through the VDU, the end-user can enter data, prepare applications programs, generate reports, perform updates to the data, modify programs, and so forth. Effectively speaking, the end-user has complete control over his or her own execution-time environment.

End-user services are initiated and managed through a control point, conceptually referred to as a "coordinator." The coordinator is responsible for establishing user facilities and providing access to them. The coordinator may be a member of the DP staff assigned to the task, may be a principal in an "information resource center" (or "solution center," as it is sometimes called), or may reside in the user environment as an experienced computer person or a computer specialist. For a first time end-user of an end-user group, the coordinator would most probably perform the following kinds of services:

- Discuss the end-user's needs, to ascertain the feasibility of matching computer facilities with the end-user's expectations.

- Establish data and report formats in conjunction with the end-user.

- Determine processing limitations.

- Prepare access codes and mechanisms.

- Assist the end-user to get the application up and running.

- Monitor the end-user's activities to ensure that the original needs are satisfied.

Once the data, application, and computed results are operational, the end-user can perform the operations mentioned previously in this section —i.e. data entry, updating, reporting, and so forth—at his or her own pace and time schedule. Storage and processing limitations may have been established by the "coordinator," but they can easily be adjusted as usage progresses. At this point, the reporting and computational structure, along with various options, is established for this particular application. It can be discussed and duly considered as a complete entity—an idea, if you will, that can be passed from person to person. In an evolutionary system, an entity of this type is known as a "meme," which is generally analogous to a gene in biology. In everyday affairs, a meme can be an idea, a concept, a tune or catch phrase, and so forth. Memes are stored in a person's memory as books in a library, and have a characteristic of passing readily between persons.

A report in the sense presented above is a *meme* for an organization and the people within it. As is common in data processing, reports have a unique property of assuming a key role far greater in significance than a stack of computer printout paper.

Here is an analogy between end-user computing and evolutionary systems. Just as concepts and ideas evolve as they are routinely accepted and circulate among various persons, so do computer reports and associated computations in an end-user environment. Because end-user software is designed for the end-user as a person, and not only for DP professionals, the end-user can make modifications to a computer application without going through the coordinator or the DP staff.

After an initial exposure to an end-user software system, an end-user can develop new applications on a need basis. The only administrative tasks involved would be to register the application with the coordinator, and establish data bases and security procedures.

The Control Point

The *control point* is an organizational mechanism designed to control the utilization of an end-user system, including hardware, software, applications, and data. Normally, the control point is staffed by one or more people, depending on the workload, with the collective responsibility for the following list of tasks:

- Collecting and anticipating user requirements for services and applications.
- End-user training and demonstrations.
- Capacity planning and performance prediction of hardware requirements to support the end-user systems.
- Dissemination of information on the end-user system.
- Evaluation of user needs.
- Data base administration.
- Consulting and user assistance.
- Establishing computer access and data base security procedures.
- Scheduling of end-user service.

- Hardware infrastructures (VDUs, communication lines, etc.).
- Determination of the level of end-user processing requirements and relevant processing limitations.
- Monitoring the operation of the end-user software in the data processing center.
- Planning and controlling recovery and backup procedures in the data processing center.

Effectively then, the control point exists as a means of assuring coordination among the persons in the end-user group, and between them and the data processing facility.

One of the primary reasons for the existence of the coordinator function is to ensure that the end-user recognizes the significance of the powerful resource at his or her disposal. In some cases, a coordinator person will emerge from the ranks of the end-user group. In others, the coordinator person will be a member of the data processing staff.

In order to fully derive the benefits to the organization of end-user computing, the coordinator person must truly believe in the concept. End-user computing will propogate within the organization through success stories, and it is the coordinator person's task to ensure that potential users are not turned off before they get started.

Within the control point, the tasks are normally divided between several persons. One person, for example, will be responsible for data base administration while another will deal with training, demonstrations, and documentation, to cite only a simple case. Clearly, one person could easily perform all coordinator tasks in a small shop.

It is also possible that each end-user could serve as his or her own control point. This option is normally open only to DP professionals, since it requires some data processing training and experience. One of the attractive features of end-user computing to many organizations is the fact that it essentially promises the benefits of computer support without data processing training. Moreover, it would destroy the advantages of end-user computing to have the end-user control his or her own environment. The end-user should really be free to concentrate on his or her own application or problem domain. It is preferable, considering the above remarks, to establish the control point on a global scale to achieve a reasonable level of productivity and overall system effectiveness.

Management's Viable Alternative

The widespread availability of microcomputers has resulted in an internal demand in many organizations for personal computing services. The inflexibility of central data processing, at least from the end-user's viewpoint, has resulted in a proliferation of small computer systems acquired to satisfy the computing and informational needs of an individual or a relatively small close-knit group of people. Spread sheet analysis, standalone word processing, and business graphics are common applications included in this domain. In some cases, data files are downloaded from a central computer to a microcomputer for local access.

A recent trend, associated with word processing systems, is related to the rapid growth of the microcomputer field. Traditionally, standalone word processing computers were available as single-purpose systems. Through the medium of standard software, many microcomputers can function as word processors at one time and personal business computers at another. This trend in the direction of multipurpose systems frequently allows data to be exchanged between office automation and data processing applications, which is an option normally provided by more comprehensive computer systems.

As a viable alternative, end-user systems can combine the power of a central computer with the convenience of a local microcomputer. The end-user's video display unit provides a window to informational resources, personal computing, and even various forms of office automation, such as word processing and electronic mail.

Organizational Dynamics

Two opposing concepts have emerged in recent years to support the end-user's need for computer services in an organizational environment. At one end of the spectrum is the "information center" concept, established logically as a centralized location, which the user can utilize for computing needs. In this case, the end-user, figuratively speaking, goes to the computer. At the opposite end of the spectrum is the notion of "bringing the computer to the user," as evidenced by the widespread use of personal business computers and end-user systems. As a matter of policy, an organization may deploy, strategically speaking, both philosophies, either collectively or by evolving from one technique to the other.

The *information center* is a structure formed within the organization where the end-user can physically locate the right people, the right equipment, and the right information to satisfy *immediate* informational and computing needs. The information center is analogous to the "war room" concept commonly used in the military and for "special projects" in the commercial world. An information center can reduce the applications backlog through the generation of ad hoc reports and other services, and it can serve as a focal point for the informational aspects of enterprise management. An information center equipped with appropriate software, terminal hardware, and graphic displays can be a reasonable option when management is faced with the problem of providing local computer service. When executives, managers, and administrators are spending an inordinate amount of time and energy on computer-related activities through the use of personal business computers and end-user systems, the establishment of an information center may be an ideal management decision. As an organizational unit, an information center can be placed within a data processing group, an office automation group, or within an administration group. This subject is covered as a separate section.

One point is unmistakeably clear. A comprehensive end-user system can satisfy the local needs of individuals and small groups, as well as the requirements of an information center. Three brief scenarios demonstrate the possibilities:

- *Case 1.* An organization can establish an information center staffed by data processing personnel, and an end-user can utilize this centralized service to obtain computational and informational results on a demand basis. The information center may be located in a central computer facility, in the end-user's general work area, or a reasonable variation thereof. Because information center personnel can utilize an end-user system, results can be obtained in a minimum time period.

- *Case 2.* An organization can establish an information center, as in case 1. As end-users become experienced in data processing concepts, there can be an evolutionary shift of developmental activity to end-user personnel. The control point, as introduced earlier, resides in the information center. This case effectively demonstrates both data processing and client centered developmental activity.

■ *Case 3.* A control point is established in the data processing or the end-user department. End-users, collectively speaking, are familiarized with the end-user system and given assistance in getting their applications up and running. As various applications mature, activity is centered in the end-user departments.

Clearly, additional options exist. For example, an information center, or its equivalent, can emerge in an end-user department. The key point, however, has been made. *The system is the solution.* Without an effective end-user system, neither data processing nor client centered developmental activity can flourish.

Escalation of Requirements

One of the most common events in data processing is the "escalation of requirements." What this is intended to mean is that the so-called demand for computational and informational services exceeds the data processing department's capacity to supply them. This is the applications backlog mentioned earlier. Many of these requirements are well founded and reflect bona fide organizational requirements. On the other hand, some of the requirements represent temporary needs, escalated into full-blown applications that are unwarranted. Here is an example of how a simple request is escalated into an unwarranted data processing requirement. An executive approaches the traditional data processing department with a loosely—formulated request for information stored in the enterprise's data base. The executive involved is not exactly sure of what he or she wants and how often, but rejects a comprehensive feasibility study because of the time and cost involved to do the work. A "quick and dirty" compromise is reached resulting in an extensive report that is generated frequently—in fact, more frequently than necessary. Subsequently, the executive refers to a few items of information from the comprehensive report on an occasional basis. It is easy to imagine how a similar requirement can be replicated many times in an organization and how a data processing facility and its staff, organized for a reasonable level of service, can be completely swamped with both a developmental and processing workload.

With an effective end-user facility, a needed report can be generated on a demand basis, and a precise set of specific needs can evolve over time without placing an unnecessary burden on the data processing department. In fact, it is often possible through end-user services to prepare a "prototype" report on the spot with lead times in minutes instead of hours, days, or weeks.

Summary

The unresolved applications backlog in the computer field is in the news these days, and it has called the computer industry's attention to a variety of nonprocedural languages and software facilities, collectively referred to as "end-user systems." The MAPPER system is a principal product in this category. The key objective of these systems is to provide fast access to informational resources and the widespread use of data manipulation facilities on a demand basis.

Informally, the end-user concept refers to the nontrivial use of computer facilities by non-DP personnel. More specifically, the end-user concept refers to three related items:

- End-user systems and languages.
- End-user application development.
- End-user open access to computer facilities.

Thus, the concept effectively puts the power of the computer into the hands of the people who will actually benefit from the increased timeliness of information and the increased productivity—that is, the end-user. An end-user system is neither demand computing nor transaction processing; it is a combination of computer hardware, software, and data communications facilities that provides the functional capability of performing traditional DP/MIS operations locally without having to utilize the services of the data processing department.

The primary advantage of end-user computing is economic, and it eventually shows up on the proverbial bottom line. Thus, the objective of end-user computing is to enhance the decision making potential of knowledge workers. The practice of placing the power of the computer into the hands of the non-DP employee clearly puts that employee into the unique position of being able to improve his or her own productivity.

The operational environment for end-user computing includes both knowledge and support workers, both of whom perform unstructured tasks established on an "as needed" basis. Workers in this class have a characteristic work pattern; they accept (or receive) input, perform analyses of various forms, and then prepare output that takes the form of person-to-person communications, reports, and various types of electronic media. Because of the widespread familiarity with computer-based information systems, including office automation, by modern knowledge and support workers, end-user computer facilities can supply a well-defined and systematic business approach to decision making and management control.

An end-user system exists as an up-to-date version of a management support system, because it supports management through local control over data and computational resources. However, an end-user system has a synergistic impact on the organization, because it marries conventional data processing and traditional MIS with the selective and extensive logical capability of the individual decision maker. The key elements in this type of management support system are:

- Who controls the information.

- Who develops the computer application.

- Who initiates the computer processing.

In an end-user system, data is extracted and summarized from conventional data processing systems, from transaction processing systems, and external sources, and it is stored as application or subject databases. Once data is prepared for an end-user group, it is essentially owned by them. Applications software is prepared by end-user personnel and executed by end-user personnel. Although end-user software may run on centralized computer facilities, it is viewed conceptually as a separate system.

Overall information systems success in an organizational setting can be achieved under the following conditions:

- Well-defined requirements are established before development activity begins.

- The end-user participates in the definition of the requirements of the object system.

- The system is related to significant business processes.
- Centralized control is established over application and subject databases.
- New applications are adequately justified.
- The end-user participates in application development and their use.

The end result of an effective information system is an enterprise-wide set of end-user developed applications that are local to a particular business unit, but span business functions and organizational boundaries when necessary.

One reason for the overall effectiveness of end-user computing is the 80–20 rule, which implies that 80 percent of the information used in a department is generated from within that department and only 20 percent comes from external sources. Conversely, 80 percent of the information processed within the department stays within the department and only 20 percent of the information will be transferred externally. The 80–20 rule is normally used to locate informational and computational resources in a distributed or end-user environment. Clearly, the economy of scale inherent in large centralized mainframe computers favors end-user computing and local control over application development.

Concepts and ideas evolve as they are routinely accepted and circulate among various persons. In an end-user environment, reports and associated computations assume a similar evolutionary characteristic. It is commonly accepted in data processing that reports have a unique property of assuming a key role greater in significance than a stack of computer printout paper.

Any resource powerful enough to influence the operation of an organization must be controlled, to a greater or lesser degree, in order to achieve coordination among the individuals involved and to ensure that standards of security and productivity are maintained. In an end-user computing environment, the control function is more technical than managerial, and provides an important link between the end-user group and the data processing facility. Control should be established on a global scale within the organization to achieve a reasonable level of overall system effectiveness.

There is an internal demand in many organizations for personal computing services. This demand results from an inflexibility of central data processing, widespread availability of microcomputers, and the phenomenal growth of office automation, especially of word processing. As a viable alternative, an end-user system can combine the power of a central computer with the convenience of a local microcomputer.

Two opposing concepts exist to support the end-user's need for computer services in an organizational setting. One concept is the information center, established as a centralized location that the user can utilize for informational and computational services. The second concept is the use of personal business computers and end-user systems to bring the computer to the person who will actually benefit from it. The information center is a centralized unit in the organization where the end-user can locate the right people, the right equipment, and the right information to resolve *immediate* informational and computing needs. An information center can reduce the applications backlog through the generation of ad hoc reports and other services, and can serve as the focal point for the informational aspects of enterprise management. The information center—equipped with appropriate software, terminal hardware, and graphic displays—can be a viable option when management is faced with the problem of providing local computer services, especially when key people are spending an inordinate amount of time and energy on computer-related activities through personal business computers and end-user systems. As informational needs are adjusted to satisfy organizational goals, end-user computing activity can evolve into the information concept though local pockets of specialization. Similarly, persons accustomed to using the services of an information center can initiate end-user computing of their own as requirements demand it.

One major problem in data processing is that simple requests often turn into big jobs. Through ad hoc reporting capability, simple requests can be handled appropriately so that organizational resources are used in a productive manner.

CHAPTER TWO

MAPPER Fundamentals

There is a growing awareness in the MIS/DP field that data structure and programming languages, as distinct disciplines, can never be totally separated. Moreover, the gradual evolution to end-user computing emphasizes the fact that in many cases, it is preferable to "show" the computer rather than to "tell" it what to do. This practice is sometimes referred to as *visual programming*. The MAPPER system provides a visual programming environment through a user-friendly report-oriented interface. The basic data structure in MAPPER is the report, which permits the end-user to deal in concrete terms with well-defined physical entities rather than abstract logical concepts. The basis for visual programming is well-established in the word processing community, where the most commonly heard maxim is, "What you see is what you get."

Introduction

As a visually-oriented report processing system, MAPPER is unique. Its origins lie in the manufacturing area and not in data processing, and this fact is perhaps evident from its "down to earth" structure and user friendliness. The MAPPER system is a user-driven facility, and many persons feel as though it could never have achieved a correspondingly high level of success if its development had been initiated by software specialists.

The name MAPPER stands for MAintaining, Preparing, and Producing Executive Reports. Literally speaking, it is not a programming language, even though it possesses a well-defined user interface. MAPPER is a total report processing system that incorporates the following elements:

- A report-oriented database.

- A set of manual user functions for performing data processing, data manipulation operations, for updating, and for reporting.

- A RUN facility for creating operational lists of MAPPER functions, similar to a macro or subroutine facility.

- A coordinator position, supported by appropriate software and procedures, that involves the general control of the MAPPER system as it relates to the design, development, and use of a report-structured data base.

Drawn from either the user domain or the data processing shop, the co-ordinator plays a key role by interfacing with DP management, user management, DP personnel, and user personnel.

Figure 2.1 gives a *Personnel Summary* in the form of a MAPPER report. All MAPPER reports have this general structure, even though the form and content vary between applications. The lines in this report are sorted by employee number. Typical MAPPER functions would be to sort the data, perhaps by employee name, and then have selected columns printed. Other representative functions would be to select certain lines —for example, all employees with a salary greater than $30,000.00—and then print selected columns, such as starting date, sex, marital status, and education. The latter example could possibly represent an elementary form of data analysis.

```
.DATE 18 MAR 83  10:34:18  RID     37    18 MAR 83
.                PERSONNEL SUMMARY
*EMPLY.   EMPLOYEE    . SOCIAL  . START.S.M.E.   .JOB.           .
* NUM .     NAME      . SEC NO  . DATE .X.S.D.DPT.CLS. SALARY    .
*=====.=============. =========. ======.=.=.=.===.===.=========.
 12097 JAMES, R.C.     116472097 600510 F W A 111 053 019758.90
 37148 THOMAS, W.W.    372587148 750815 M M D 557 010 057900.00
 42635 BORDER, S.K.    491392635 630220 M D M 557 017 036500.00
 48113 WILLIAMS, T.C.  491638113 470615 M M M 111 001 131690.00
 69902 ASHEN, P.C.     658219902 551201 F M A 237 053 023614.50
 74257 CARTER, J.A.    724474257 590610 M S M 111 002 095000.00
 80392 RICHARDS, D.K.  813120392 710716 F S B 415 011 029317.75
 87613 WATSON, H.T.    885747613 830103 F S B 639 014 027500.00
              ..... END REPORT .....
```

Figure 2.1 *Personnel Summary* in the form of a MAPPER report.

A definitive characteristic of the MAPPER system is that the end-user can enter commands manually and the result is displayed immediately, in real time. While this is a noteworthy feature, there is clearly a limit to what can be done manually, from the standpoint of both efficiency and user capability. It either takes too long or the user does not have the background to do it, and you do not want to have a highly-paid person entering commands repetitively. This is where the RUN facility comes in. An experienced person makes a RUN, composed of MAPPER commands and probably options and logical capability, and gives it a name. From then on, it can be used as though it were a built-in MAPPER command.

The MAPPER coordination job is indispensable in a well-run data processing shop, because it serves as a control point through which the impact of MAPPER on the organization can be assessed. The coordinator is not only concerned with facilities management, but additionally with data security, database design and operation, and cost-effective MAPPER applications.

MAPPER Database Structure

A database in MAPPER is structured into modes, types, and reports. An informational dialogue always takes place in terms of reports, called RIDs, for reasons given below, but the primary access mechanism is through modes for data security and types for data organization.

Through a password system, a user can access a mode—analogous in concept to a filing cabinet to which a person has an appropriate key. Within each mode there exist distinct types, corresponding in principle to a drawer of a file cabinet. Within each type there exist reports of the same format, similar in concept to a file folder. The analogy between MAPPER database structure and a manual filing system is summarized as follows:

MAPPER Database Structure	Manual Filing System
Mode ⟷	Filing Cabinet
Type ⟷	File Drawer
Report ⟷	File Folder

There can be eight distinct types within a mode, designated by the letters B through I and called *formed reports*. Each report within a type has the same form, which refers to the fact that the data organization and column headings are the same. As would be expected, the data within various reports in a formed report type are not the same. A new report can be "cloned" from an existing report, and it will have the same form as its master.

Mode Pairs

Each *mode* is identified and referenced by a "mode pair," referring to a set of even/odd numbers, such as 0/1, 36/37, 62/63, or 118/119. Each even/odd pair is associated with the same data, and the "evenness" or "oddness" of a number denotes its access privilege, delineated as follows:

> Even Mode ———→ Read/Write Access
> Odd Mode ———→ Read Only Access

A user's mode is established when he or she is registered as a user in the access tables of the MAPPER system.

Modes are normally assigned to a department, and clearly some departments will require more than one mode. Thus, a user may have access to more than one mode on an intradepartmental or interdepartmental basis.

Report Identification

As covered above, reports are organized within types, which are represented in each even/odd mode. Each report in MAPPER is uniquely identified by Report IDentification number, referred to as a RID. A representative RID number is 4C, meaning report numbered 4 in type C. A report identified by 4C can exist in several modes, and thus the code may denote different reports.

Through usage, the acronym RID has become synonomous in MAPPER circles with the word "report." Thus, a person may say, for example, "Put RID 4C on the screen." This would be an abbreviated way of saying, "Put report identified by RID number 4C on the screen." In fact, MAPPER people customarily refer to RIDs instead of reports.

The organization of RIDs within a mode set can be conceptualized as follows:

Mode set $m/m+1$
Type B Reports
RID 1B
RID 2B
RID 3B
RID nB
Type C Reports
RID 1C
RID 2C
RID 3C
RID nC
And so forth
for Types
D through I

where $m/m+1$ is an even/odd pair of numbers, such as 218/219.

RID numbers are assigned consecutively by the MAPPER system, starting with the number 1 within each mode and type. When a report is deleted, its number is reassigned during the next request. This subject is covered in following sections.

Report Definition

The manner in which reports are defined in MAPPER is amazingly simple; in fact, it is so straightforward that its power is often overlooked. When a report is registered with the coordinator, a report structure and column

```
Report    *EMPLY.    EMPLOYEE    . SOCIAL    . START.S.M.E.    .JOB.
Format    * NUM .      NAME      . SEC NO    . DATE .X.S.D.DPT.CLS. SALARY .
          *====== ================ ========== ====== = = = === === ========
   1         X            X            X         X   X X X  X    X        X
   2         X            X                                 X    X
   3                                             X   X X X       X        X
   .
   .
   .
            There are 6 possible formats for each type
```

Figure 2.2 *Conceptual* view of how report formats are defined.

headings are established. Up to six formats can be indicated, as suggested by Figure 2.2. A format number can be specified, and when the report is displayed, the particular set of columns is generated. Effectively, the over-all report structure is the report's *format*, and a specific set of columns and headings is known as its *subformat*. The manner in which a subformat is specified is covered in a subsequent section entitled, "Control Line."

Report Creation

There are a variety of ways that a report can be created in the MAPPER system. An explicit distinction is made here between a "model report," which gives its structure (i.e. its format) and its subformats, and an instance of the report in which data can be stored. The model report is a template for physical occurrences of that report type, and is called an *experimental report.*

The most frequently used commands for this purpose are the Add Report (AR), Duplicate Report (XR), and Replace Report (REP) commands. When a report is created, it need not necessarily contain any data; but of course, it almost always will. There are several commands, such as add and delete lines, that permit the contents of a report to be manipulated.

Line Size

When a report is defined as a collaborative effort between a user and the coordinator, a line size is implicitly established through the specification of fields and column headings. Two line sizes are recognized:

> 80 length: 1–80 characters
> 132 length: 81–132 characters

All lines in a report have the same length. All reports in a type have the same line length.

When a subformat is used to display a report, only the display operation is affected by the structure of the subformat. The original report remains intact and its line length is invariant.

Characteristics of a Type

All RIDs—to use MAPPER terminology—in a type have the same fields, the same line lengths, the same editing, the same predefined lines (i.e. the headings), and the same subformats.

One important characteristic of a type is a specification of the editing that is performed when a line is displayed. In column formed lines, edit choices are available for each character position of a field. Some of the edit choices that are available are numeric, alphabetic, content, blank, and data-defined fields. This facility permits the MAPPER system to verify the kind of data that is entered into a character position. Through data-defined fields, system calls can be initiated to place current data, such as a date or time, into prespecified fields.

Other kinds of lines are permitted in MAPPER, such as headings, dates, and so forth. A "free form" data line is also defined; it has special characteristics.

Free-Form Lines

In addition to types B through I, each user has access to a general type, known as type A, that is shared among all modes. Type A data is free form and is limited to possessing 80 character line lengths. A type A data line always starts with a period (.) in column one. Because type A reports can be accessed from any mode in MAPPER, there is no data security with them. Sensitive free-form data should be placed in types B through I using a corresponding free-form line.

Types of Lines in MAPPER

A report in MAPPER can be constructed from the following types of lines:

- Column-formed lines that begin with a tab set character and contain data that can be edited.

- Column-formed lines that do not begin with a tab set character or a period or an asterisk, and contain data that can be edited.

- Column-formed lines that begin with an asterisk and do not contain data.

- Free-form lines that begin with a period and represent comment lines and free-form data.

The first, third, and fourth line types are demonstrated in Figure 2.1.

The "tab set" line is of particular importance since most MAPPER data is stored in this form. The tab set character is printed, but is placed in column one and between data fields. The terminal character in a line is also a tab character. The tab characters are an operational convenience and are normally not a major concern in report processing. The column-formed line that does not begin with a tab character is a closely related format. In this line type (referred to as a "non-tab" line), the initial characters A through Z, and tab characters separate the data fields, as in the previous case. In both of these line types, data is edited when it is placed in a field, and the report can be "shifted." *Shifting* refers to horizontal scrolling when the horizontal width of the report is greater than the screen size. In general, column-formed lines can be shifted. It should be emphasized that column-formed data is not restricted to numeric information. Column-formed data may include alphabetic characters, numeric characters, and special characters—provided that editing capability is established accordingly.

Lines that begin with an asterisk (*) character are normally used for column headings, but can be used as trailer lines, as well. This topic is discussed further. Asterisk lines are column formed and can be shifted with their respective columns. Asterisk lines are not edited, because report data is not moved into them. All column-formed lines (i.e. tab, non-tab, and asterisk) can be up to 132 characters in length, hence the need to be shiftable for conventional display screens.

Lines that begin with a period (.) are intended for report heading, comment, and free-form lines. The length of this type of line is limited to 80 characters and the line is not shiftable.

Each type of line has a particular purpose in a MAPPER report. This subject is covered next.

Report Structure

Most reports in MAPPER look pretty much the same, even though there are probably enough exceptions to make a liar out of almost anyone. Nevertheless, the level of similarity permits the various sections of a report to be identified. Again, Figure 2.1 can be used as a model. The following sections are listed:

- The date line.
- The title line.
- Header lines.
- Data lines.
- "End Report" line.

The *date line* is a period line that begins with the word DATE, followed by the following items reading from left to right:

- Date of last update.
- RID number.
- Date the report was created.
- The user ID of the last person who updated the report.

The data line is not solely intended for informational purposes. The last update and creation dates are used for cleansing the MAPPER system on a periodic basis.

The *title line* gives the report title and always follows the date line. At the right of the line is the report type (e.g. type B in Figure 2.1) and an octal number used internally to represent the mode and type.

Header lines follow title lines. They are column-formed and begin with an asterisk. Periods are used as field separators, and equal signs (=) are used to separate column headings from data.

An established MAPPER convention is that the first data line is line 6. This leaves room for a date line, a title line, and three header lines. A maximum of three period and five asterisk lines can be used.

Data lines are tab lines, non-tab lines, asterisk lines, and period lines. When asterisk and period lines are used in the body of a report, they must follow tab-set column-formed lines as trailer lines. A report may include blank lines in the beginning, interspersed in the body of the report, or at its end. A MAPPER report may contain no lines at all or only blank lines. In fact, one of the latter conditions may reflect the state of a report just after it was created.

All MAPPER reports end with the .... END REPORT .... line.

Line Hierarchy

In many information systems applications, it is desirable to incorporate descriptive information following column-formed edited data. Typical examples would be financial reporting, inventory systems, and medical/patient records. A hierarchy of line types exists in MAPPER in the following order:

- Column-formed lines starting with the tab character.
- Asterisk lines.
- Comment lines.
- Column-formed lines not starting with the tab character.

Here is the way that the line hierarchy works. If asterisk or comment lines are placed in a report after a column-formed line starting with a tab character, the asterisk and comment lines will follow the edited line in report processing, as in the case of a sort operation. Asterisk and comment lines used in this manner are called *trailer lines.*

Trailer lines may not be used with column-formed lines that do not start with the tab character. Moreover, this type of line may not be used as a trailer line.

Control Line

The screen format in the MAPPER system is designed to give the user complete information on the status of the system and control over its operation. When a report is displayed on the screen, the date line is actually the second line on the screen, even though it is known as line 1. There is a line 0.

The first line on the screen is called "line 0," or alternatively the *control line.* The control line gives the report status, vis-a-vis its display format, and permits horizontal or vertical positioning of the report on the screen. Figure 2.3 shows the report given previously, with the control line added. The entries in the control line are given as follows:

LINE> *u* FMT> *u* RL> *u* SHFT> *u* HLD CHRS> *u* HLD LN> *u* > *s* >

where *u* denotes a position for user input or system output, and *s* represents status information. The spacing in the control line in the text is not accurate; however, the spacing in Figure 2.3 is realistic. The keywords LINE, FMT, RL, SHFT, HLD CHRS, and HLD LN signify special indicators, described as follows:

Keyword	Meaning
LINE	The line number, in the report, of the first line held on the screen.
FMT	The number of the subformat for the report that is on the screen.
RL	The number of lines that the report is scrolled vertically. A plus sign or blank denotes up; a minus sign denotes down.
SHFT	The number of characters that the report is scrolled horizontally. A plus sign or blank denotes left; a minus sign denotes right.
HLD CHRS	The number of characters to be held on the left edge of the screen.
HLD LN	The number of lines to be held on the top of the screen.

```
LINE  1      FMT     RL        SHFT       HLD CHRS     HLD LN       fcs
.DATE 18 MAR 83  10:34:18  RID      37    18 MAR 83
.                         PERSONNEL SUMMARY
*EMPLY.    EMPLOYEE  . SOCIAL  . START.S.M.E.   .JOB.            .
* NUM .     NAME     . SEC NO  . DATE .X.S.D.DPT.CLS. SALARY     .
*=====.===============.==========.=======.=.=.=.===.===.=========.
 12097 JAMES, R.C.     116472097 600510 F W A 111 053 019758.90
 37148 THOMAS, W.W.    372587148 750815 M M D 557 010 057900.00
 42635 BORDER, S.K.    491392635 630220 M D M 557 017 036500.00
 48113 WILLIAMS, T.C.  491638113 470615 M M M 111 001 131690.00
 69902 ASHEN, P.C.     658219902 551201 F M A 237 053 023614.50
 74257 CARTER, J.A.    724474257 590610 M S M 111 002 095000.00
 80392 RICHARDS, D.K.  813120392 710716 F S B 415 011 029317.75
 87613 WATSON, H.T.    885747613 830103 F S B 639 014 027500.00
                        ..... END REPORT .....
```

Figure 2.3 Control line (displayed above the date line in the Personnel Summary report).

The status information denoted by *s* at the right of the control line concerns the MAPPER character set and the result created by MAPPER. The status indications most normally generated are:

Indicator	Meaning
FCS	The report is displayed in the full character set.
LCS	The report is displayed in the limited character set.
FCSU	The report is displayed in the full character set, upper case.
RESULT	The report is a result created by a MAPPER command.
UPD RESULT	The report is a result created by a MAPPER update command.

The keywords can be used to control screen operations as described in the following paragraphs.

The LINE position in the control line is used to position the screen to a specific line. To display a particular line as the first line on the screen, the requested line number should be entered in the LINE field and the entry should be transmitted to the computer. MAPPER will respond by displaying the report with the specified line in line 1 of the screen. By entering a line number greater than the report size, such as 9999, the last line of the report is displayed. When line number 1 is entered, the first line of the report is displayed.

The FMT position in the control line is used to display a report in one of its subformats. To utilize the FMT field, the report must be on the screen. The subformat number is entered in the FMT field and the entry is transmitted to the computer. MAPPER responds to the request by displaying the report in the subformat indicated.

The RL position in the control line is used to roll the contents of the screen forward or backward. To roll the screen, a positive or negative number is entered into the RL field and the entry is transmitted to the computer. If the number is positive, the report is rolled forward that many lines. If the number is negative, the report is rolled backward that many lines. Once a number is entered and transmitted, a roll direction is established. To roll the report by one screenful in the established direction, all the user need do is to move the cursor to the RL field and transmit. The LINE field operates in conjunction with the RL keyword by reflecting the current line number.

The SHFT position in the control line is used to shift the contents of the screen horizontally. To shift the screen, a positive or negative number is entered into the SHFT field and the entry is transmitted to the computer. If a positive number is entered, the report is moved the indicated number of characters to the left of the screen; or alternately, the screen is moved to the right over the report. If a negative number is entered, the report is moved to the right. Comment lines, i.e. lines that begin with a period, are not shiftable. Shifting pertains to character columns and not data columns. To shift the report one character to the left on the screen, the cursor should be moved to the SHFT field, and either a plus sign, a +1, or nothing can be entered and the entry is transmitted to the computer. Similarly, a right shift of one character position can be achieved with a simple minus sign or a −1 entry.

When a report is scrolled up on the screen, the column headings are normally lost and the identity of the various data columns can easily be confused. Through the HLD LN keyword, a specified number of lines can be held on the top of the screen. To use this option, a positive number should be entered into the HLD LN field. After the value is transmitted to the computer, the report can be rolled up or down with the RL keyword and the held lines are fixed on the top of the screen.

Characters can also be held on the left edge of the screen with the HLD CHRS keyword. After a positive number is entered and transmitted to the computer, the specified number of character columns are held on the screen.

A user-friendly screen management technique is mandatory for an effective end-user computing system. The "control line" concept is notable in this regard. Through a fast-access form of user interaction, the process of screen management can be further simplified.

Sign-On and the MAPPER Logo

After a terminal connection is made to the MAPPER system and before sign on, a *station idle* logo is displayed, as demonstated in Figure 2.4.

```
******** DATA PROCESSING ********
*   THE  M A P P E R  SYSTEM    *
* UNIT: 123  USER:       <IDLE> *
*********  LEVEL 99R9    *********
```

Figure 2.4 Representative MAPPER station idle logo.

The station idle presents the following information: terminal unit, installation identification, and system level.

The sign-on procedure needed to use the MAPPER system requires a user identification, a department number, and an optional password. The sign-on line takes the following form:

]user-id, department-number, password

where "]" is a closing bracket. Representative sign-on lines are:

]JAMES,37,UBS
]ROGERS,130,KATHY
]AUTRY,76

In the latter case, a password is not required for sign-on. To add a password, the following form is used:

]user-id,department-number/password

as in:

]AUTRY, 76/CHAMPION

Following this entry, the password CHAMPION is required for subsequent sign-ons. The form needed to change a password is:

]user-id,department-number,old/new

as in:

]AUTRY,76,CHAMPION/SCOUT

As a result of the last sign-on, the password SCOUT is required.

It is also possible to establish a coded password that can change with the month, day, time, or station number. Coded passwords are more complicated than the simple kind, and a MAPPER reference manual can be consulted in this regard.

The sign-on procedure is entered, as shown in Figure 2.5, resulting in the *active system* logo, depicted in Figure 2.6. This logo gives the user identification and the registered mode to which the user has access.

```
]AUTRY,76,SCOUT

        ******** DATA PROCESSING ********
        *    THE  M A P P E R  SYSTEM   *
        * UNIT:  123  USER:       <IDLE> *
        **********  LEVEL 99R9   *********
```

Figure 2.5 Sign-on.

```
xxxxxxxx DATA PROCESSING xxxxxxxxx
x   THE  M A P P E R  SYSTEM    x
x UNIT: 123   USER:     `AUTRY` x
xxxxxxx MODE  99 DATA BASE xxxxxxx
```

Figure 2.6 Representative MAPPER Active System Logo.

Sign-Off

Once a dialogue is established between a user and the MAPPER system, the user may access all database facilities that are authorized. When a MAPPER session has been completed, the terminal should be released to protect the data in the system. This is achieved by entering the letter X in the control line and transmitting it to the computer. MAPPER responds with the station idle logo.

Summary

The practice of showing the computer what to do rather than telling it is sometimes referred to as visual programming. Through a concrete user-friendly report-oriented interface, the MAPPER system provides such a visual programming environment. The concepts are well established in the word processing community.

The name MAPPER, which is an acronym for MAintaining, Preparing, and Producing Executive Reports, is a total report processing system that incorporates the following elements:

- A reporting database.
- A set of manual user functions.
- A RUN facility.
- A coordinator position.

MAPPER is a systems solution to the DP/MIS reporting problem, and the above elements emphasize the fact that it represents an organizational facility and not a personal tool. A definitive characteristic of the MAPPER system is that the end-user can enter commands manually and the result is displayed immediately, in real time. Through the RUN facility, an experienced person can construct a set of MAPPER commands and logical options, and assign it a name for use as though it were a built-in MAPPER command. The coordinator serves as a control point through which the impact of MAPPER on the total organization can be assessed.

A MAPPER database is structured into modes, types, and reports, and an analogy can be drawn between a manual filing system and a MAPPER database as follows:

MAPPER Database Structure	Manual Filing System
Mode ⟷	Filing Cabinet
Type ⟷	File Drawer
Report ⟷	File Folder

There can be eight distinct types within a mode, identified by the letters B through I. All reports within a given type have the same form. The access level to MAPPER is through a mode, assigned to a user or department, and password protected.

Each mode is assigned a mode pair, referring to a set of even/odd numbers, such as 62/63. Each even/odd pair is associated with the same data, and the "evenness" or "oddness" of a number denotes its access privilege: an even mode indicates read/write access, and an odd mode is restricted to read only access.

Within a type, a report is uniquely identified by a Report IDentification number, referred to as its RID. A typical RID is 23C, denoting report numbered 23 in type C. Reports are customarily called RIDs. RID numbers are assigned consecutively within a type by the MAPPER system.

A report is defined when it is registered by the user with the coordinator. At that time, a report structure, column headings, and subformats are established. Up to six subformats can be specified as display options.

A logical template for each report type, termed an experimental report, is established in MAPPER. When a physical occurrence of a report is desired, its structure is determined through the use of the template. The most widely used commands for creating reports are Add Report (AR), Duplicate Report (XR), and Replace Report (REP).

An important attribute of a report is its line size and all reports in a type have the same size. Two line sizes are recognized:

80 length: 1–80 characters
132 length: 81–132 characters

When a subformat is used to display a report, only the display operation is affected by the structure of the subformat. The original report remains intact, and its line length is invariant.

All RIDs in a type have the same fields, same line lengths, editing, column headings, and subformats. Edit choices are available for each character position of a field; this feature allows MAPPER to verify the type of data that is entered into a field.

Each mode also contains type A data that is shared among all modes on a system-wide basis. Type A data is free form.

The data lines in a MAPPER report can be constructed from column formed lines and free form lines. Column formed lines can begin with a tab set character, without a tab set character, and with an asterisk. Asterisk lines are normally used as column headings. Characteristics of the various line types are summarized as follows:

Line Type	Column Formed	Edited	Shiftable	Length
Tab set	Yes	Yes	Yes	80–132
Non-tab set	Yes	Yes	Yes	80–132
Asterisk	Yes	Yes	Yes	80–132
Period	No	No	No	80

Reports comprise several well-defined sections:

- Date line.
- Title line.
- Header line.
- Data lines.
- End report line.

The date and title lines describe the report and operational environment. A hierarchy of line types exists in MAPPER in the following order:

- Tab set column-formed edited lines.
- Asterisk column-formed non-edited lines.
- Comment lines.
- Non-tab set column-formed edited lines.

Using the hierarchy, asterisk and comment lines follow a tab-set line in report processing when it is moved, as in a sort operation. Asterisk and comment lines, used in this manner, are called trailer lines. The concept does not apply to non-tab set lines.

The control line, which is the first non-report line on the screen, or line 0, is designed to give the user complete information on the status of the MAPPER system and control over its operation. The entries in the control line have the following keywords: LINE, FMT, RL, SHFT, HLD CHRS, and HLD LN. The LINE position in the control line is used to position the screen to a specific line. The FMT position in the control line is used to display a report in one of its subformats. The RL position in the control line is used to roll the contents of the screen forward or backward. The SHFT position in the control line is used to shift the contents of the screen horizontally. With the HLD LN keyword, a specified number of lines can be held on the top of the screen, and similarly, the HLD CHRS key permits characters to be held on the left edge of the screen. The HLD LN is normally used to sustain a column heading while the HLD CHRS can be used to keep a column of descriptive information.

The sign-on procedure for using the MAPPER system provides a level of security that requires a user identification, department number, and password to be specified. A sample sign-on line is:

]AUTRY, 76/CHAMPION

A sophisticated form of coded passwords that uses current values, such as time, day, or date, is also available.

The MAPPER system uses a characteristic logo to provide definitive information to the user before and after sign-on. An idle logo is used prior to sign on, giving only the terminal identification, installation, and system level. After sign on, the active logo displays the user identification and the mode to which the user has access.

A sign-off from MAPPER is advisable for data security, and is achieved by placing an X in the control line and transmitting it to the computer. The MAPPER system responds to a sign-off with an idle logo.

CHAPTER THREE

Access and Modification Functions

The effectiveness of an end-user computing system is inherent in the facilities that permit a user to access the system and generate needed results without requiring the services of a day-to-day computer specialist. If accessed on a daily basis, almost any system can be used with skill and dexterity. But, when a system is to be accessed by nonspecialists or by occasional users, then an important attribute, generally classified as "user friendliness," is needed. Through its report-oriented user interface, MAPPER goes a long way toward providing a user-friendly system. However, the capability of easily referencing a report, and then being able to conveniently change fields, lines, and large data units, is also mandatory for any system in order to be classed as user-friendly. MAPPER is user-friendly.

Introduction

Access and modification functions in MAPPER are conveniently classed as service functions, line-oriented functions, and report-oriented functions. The objective of the service functions is to get an end-user up and running, in any terminal session, as quickly as possible. The objective of the line-oriented functions is to allow the user to make local changes to reports by visually changing the data on the screen. The objective of report-oriented functions is to manipulate reports on a global basis by dealing with a report as a unified data structure. Table 3.1 gives a brief summarization of the access and modification functions covered here.

Table 3.1 Access and Modification Functions

Service Functions

FUNction

HELP

Type

Mode change

Display report

Fast access

Abort

Release

Line-Oriented Functions

Update line

Add line

Duplicate line

Delete line

Report-Oriented Functions

Add report

Duplicate report

Delete report

Replace report

Add on report

Add to report

Print report

Service Functions

For the occasional or beginning user of MAPPER, it is often convenient to have a simple way of jogging one's memory about the most frequently

```
*_**************** MAPPER FUNCTIONS *************************
* M       MODE SELECTION          AR(XR)   ADD/DUP REPORT   *
* D       DISPLAY REPORT          DR       DELETE REPORT    *
* L       LINE CONTROL RESTORE    AUX      COP/CASSETTE/VIP *
* S,SU    SEARCH (SEARCH UPDATE)  I        INDEX FORM TYPE  *
* F       FIND REPORT DATA REQUEST TOT     TOTALIZE REQUEST *
* PR      PRINT REQUEST           ADON(ADTO) APPEND REPORTS *
* T       DISPLAY TYPES IN MODE   LOC(CHG) LOCATE (CHANGE)  *
* X       RELEASE USER I.D.       START(RET) BATCH START/RET*
* SORT    SORT REQUEST            A        ARITHMETIC       *
* DATE    DATE ANALYSIS REQUEST   MA(MAU)  MATCH(MATCH UPD) *
```

Figure 3.1 The most commonly used commands generated with the FUN keyword.

used MAPPER commands and their keywords. Nothing could be more convenient than to use MAPPER itself for this purpose. The most common functions in MAPPER can be listed by entering the keyword FUN in the control line and transmitting it to the computer. The MAPPER system responds with the screen given in Figure 3.1. For a more detailed description of the various options available to a user, the HELP command or the MAPPER reference manual should be consulted.

The keyword HELP is an industry standard for online assistance facilities. The MAPPER system incorporates a multi-level help quality to provide all of the detailed information necessary for using the system. To obtain help from MAPPER, the user need only enter the keyword HELP in the control line and transmit it to the computer. The computer responds with a screen similar to that given in Figure 3.2. The cursor is placed in the ROLL position so the user may conveniently scroll through the entire help report.

To obtain additional levels of detail, the user must move the cursor to the desired line, such as Display Report (D), and transmit that line to the computer. MAPPER responds with a more detailed description, including necessary formats and requirements, as demonstrated in Figure 3.3. Some descriptions include several levels of detail.

Most books, reports, and other documents contain a table of contents providing a preview of the information contained therein. MAPPER is no exception to this convention; the Type command can be used to list the form types in a user's mode. Figure 3.4 gives an example. To obtain a list of the form types in a mode, the user should enter the letter T in the control line and transmit it to the computer.

```
        ****    SYSTEM INFORMATION   ****
                ROLL     (enter SYSTEM target if known)
    TARGET                       EXPLANATION
============   =========================================================
A             FORTRAN BASED ARITHMETIC CALCULATOR
ABORT         ABORT AN IN PROCESS OPERATION
ADON          APPEND A REPORT TO THE DISPLAYED REPORT
ADTO          APPEND DISPLAYED REPORT TO ANOTHER REPORT
APPL          APPLICATION DESIGN CONCERNS
AR            ADD A REPORT
AUX           SEND REPORTS TO AUXILIARY DEVICES
BASE          MAPPER 1100 DATA BASE
BF            BINARY FIND
BPORT         BATCH PORT AND BATCH PORT ERROR HANDLING
CAL           CALCULATE REPORT VALUES
CC            REPORT COLUMN COUNTER RUN FUNCTION
CHG           CHANGE A CHARACTER STRING
CONTROL       DESCRIPTION OF MAPPER CONTROL LINE
COP           AUXILIARY PRINT RUN FUNCTION
COPY          COPY FILES FROM SYSTEM TO SYSTEM
CUR           TAPE CASSETTE UTILITY RUN FUNCTION
CUT           CUT/PASTE FUNCTION
D             DISPLAY A REPORT
DATE          ANALYZE DATES WITHIN A REPORT
```

Figure 3.2 Initial screen from the HELP command.

A mode change can be executed by a signed-on MAPPER user, provided that a corresponding access privilege is registered in the system. To change modes the user need only enter a command of the form:

M new-mode password

where "new mode" is the mode number to which the user desires access, and "password" is the registered password of that mode. The following example demonstrates the concept:

M 134 MABLE

In this case, 134 is the new mode number and MABLE is the password. If the user has been granted access to the specified mode or the mode has a blanket access, and the given password is valid, a mode switch is performed.

The most widely used command in MAPPER is probably Display Report (D), because of the visual fidelity it provides for the other access and modification functions. To display a report the user should enter the letter D in the control line and transmit it to the computer; MAPPER responds with the following script:

DISPLAY REPORT
    RID   ,
    TYPE   ,

```
.DATE 18 MAR 83  11:03:18     REPORT GENERATION
                         MAPPER 1100 ONLINE SYSTEM RESPONSE
             ** To return from HELP, press F1 or enter RSM and transmit. **
              Do not XR this result. It will end up in a restricted mode.
DOCUMENT-SYSTEM             REV. 8.6              MAPPER 1100

DISPLAY REPORT FUNCTION
-----------------------

DESCRIPTION:

The display function displays a MAPPER 1100 report.

REQUEST:

Enter a D in the control line and transmit to receive the display function
request mask.

                    DISPLAY REPORT

                        RID      ,
                        TYPE  ,

Enter the report identifier (RID) number in the RID field and the alphabetic
letter code in the type field and transmit.

  In the following example a display of RID 1a is being requested

                    DISPLAY REPORT

                        RID 1       ,
                        TYPE a ,

RESULT:       Report 1a will be displayed on the terminal.
There is a fast access method of displaying a report. In the control line enter
RID-TYPE. Where RID = the RID number and type = the alpha type (a thru i)
For example: 2b followed by a transmit will cause the MAPPER system to display
report 2b of the mode you are currently in.

DISPLAY FUNCTION SYSTEM MESSAGES
================================

The DISPLAY function does not have any specific messages, but uses many of
the miscellaneous messages as described in the help target misc.
                    ..... END REPORT .....
```

Figure 3.3 Additional levels of the help facility demonstrated for the
          Display Report (D) command.

```
--------------- RELATIVE MODE 16/17 REPORT FORM TYPES  --------------
.C.        FORM TYPE       . FORM .C.        FORM TYPE       . FORM .
.D.        DESCRIPTION     . TYPE .D.        DESCRIPTION     . TYPE .
.=.=====================.======.=.=====================.=====.
 B PRODUCTION STATUS       000202 F FULL CHAR.U&L FREE FORM  000212
 C FACTOR BASE             000204 G RUN FUNCTION DATA FCS    000214
 D ORDER STATUS            000206 H WORD PROCESSING REPORTS  000216
 E DEMO RUN FUNCTIONS      000210 I EXPERIMENTAL REPORTS     000220
```

Figure 3.4 Example of form types in a mode generated with the
           Type command.

After manually inserting the requested information such as

DISPLAY REPORT

RID 2   ,
TYPE B,

the user transmits the entire screen to the computer. MAPPER then displays the requested report, as demonstrated previously.

Because of a high-level of utilization of this and other widely used MAPPER commands, a *fast access* method is available. To avoid the script, all the user need do is enter the RID number, followed by the type designation anywhere in the control line, and transmit it to the computer. MAPPER then displays the report without requiring further user interaction. Most commands in MAPPER have fast access counterparts, even though all of them are not covered here.

Two MAPPER functions permit ongoing operations to be terminated. The *abort function* can be used to terminate the execution of a command that was inappropriately entered. Typical examples are the sort and search commands, because they usually consume time and computer resources. A function can be aborted while in progress by pressing the Message Waiting (MSG WAIT) key on the keyboard of a Sperry Univac terminal. On other equipment, a "cancel" key is commonly used for this purpose.

The *release function* deletes a report present on the screen and displays the active system logo. To release a report, a carat character (^) should be entered *anywhere* on the screen and transmitted to the computer. Clearly, this function should not be used solely to clear the screen, since it puts the system in a pristine state and intermediate results are lost. Specific terminal-oriented functions are available to simply clear the screen, such as moving the cursor to the home position and erasing to the end of the file.

Operational Philosophy of MAPPER

The fundamental operational philosophy of MAPPER is that modifications can be made to reports displayed on the screen, and they are reflected in the associated data file on a mass storage device. In reality, however, an update-in-place is not performed, even though the end-user is given the operational illusion that it is actually happening. Changes are written to an update file, known as MAPER0, and the original files are updated in a special post mortem run. The first time a report is updated (i.e. data values are entered, changed, or deleted) and any time a line or report-oriented function changes the size of the report, the entire report is written to the data file name MAPER0. For subsequent updates, only changed lines are written to MAPER0. However, if the size of the report is subsequently changed, then the entire report is again written to MAPER0. After a change of any kind is made to a report, a flag is set in MAPPER's internal tables. Prior to the setting of the flag, references are made to the original copy. After the flag is set, references are made to MAPER0. The post mortem run, mentioned above, performs reconciliation and consolidation operations on a scheduled periodic basis.

Line-Oriented Functions

The procedure for changing a field, a line, or any number of lines of a report in MAPPER is a visual operation, performed as follows:

- The report is displayed on the screen.
- Rolling and shifting are performed if the proper fields are not displayed.
- A Start-of-Entry Character (▶) is placed before the change.
- A screen update is entered.

When the change is transmitted to the computer, the information between the Start-of-Entry (SOE) and the cursor are written to MAPER0. The screen is already changed by the manual operation. This operation and the final result are demonstrated in Figure 3.5. Several fields and lines can be updated in one transmission, provided that all changes lie between the Start of Entry and the Cursor. It is generally recommended to place the ▶ and ■ brackets only around the changes, because MAPER0 can be filled quickly if the Start of Entry Character (▶) is always placed at the beginning of the report.

If an error is made during screen update and before transmission, the screen can be repainted to display its original contents. To repaint the screen, the cursor should be moved to the control line, and the command

```
.DATE 18 MAR 83  11:07:49  RID     37    18 MAR 83
.                 PERSONNEL SUMMARY
*EMPLY.   EMPLOYEE   . SOCIAL  . START.S.M.E.   .JOB.          .
* NUM .    NAME      . SEC NO  . DATE .X.S.D.DPT.CLS. SALARY   .
*=====.==============.=========.======.=.=.=.===.===.=========.
 12097 JAMES, R.C.    116472097 600510 F W A 111 053 019758.90
 37148 THOMAS, W.W.  ▶ 111111111■750815 M M D 557 010 057900.00
 42635 BORDER, S.K.   491392635 630220 M D M 557 017 036500.00
 48113 WILLIAMS, T.C. 491638113 470615 M M M 111 001 131690.00
 69902 ASHEN, P.C.    658219902 551201 F M A 237 053 023614.50
 74257 CARTER, J.A.   724474257 590610 M S M 111 002 095000.00
 80392 RICHARDS, D.K. 813120392 710716 F S B 415 011 029317.75
 87613 WATSON, H.T.   885747613 830103 F S B 639 014 027500.00
                      ..... END REPORT .....
```

(a) Procedure.

```
.DATE 18 MAR 83  11:07:49  RID     37    18 MAR 83
.                 PERSONNEL SUMMARY
*EMPLY.   EMPLOYEE   . SOCIAL  . START.S.M.E.   .JOB.          .
* NUM .    NAME      . SEC NO  . DATE .X.S.D.DPT.CLS. SALARY   .
*=====.==============.=========.======.=.=.=.===.===.=========.
 12097 JAMES, R.C.    116472097 600510 F W A 111 053 019758.90
 37148 THOMAS, W.W.   111111111 750815 M M D 557 010 057900.00
 42635 BORDER, S.K.   491392635 630220 M D M 557 017 036500.00
 48113 WILLIAMS, T.C. 491638113 470615 M M M 111 001 131690.00
 69902 ASHEN, P.C.    658219902 551201 F M A 237 053 023614.50
 74257 CARTER, J.A.   724474257 590610 M S M 111 002 095000.00
 80392 RICHARDS, D.K. 813120392 710716 F S B 415 011 029317.75
 87613 WATSON, H.T.   885747613 830103 F S B 639 014 027500.00
                      ..... END REPORT .....
```

(b) Result.

Figure 3.5 Line Modification. Note Start-of-Entry (▶) and Cursor (■)
          characters.

PNT (for Paint) should be transmitted to the computer. The screen will be refreshed, and the update or entry operation can be started over.

The procedure for adding lines to a report entails the following steps:

- Display the report.

- Move the cursor to the line after which lines should be added.

- Erase that line.

- Enter the following sequence of symbols:

    ▶] n+

    where: ▶ is the Start-of-Entry character.
           ] is the closing bracket.
           n is the number of lines to be added.
           + is a plus sign, meaning "add lines".

■ Transmit the entry to the computer.

At that point, the report will be opened up to reveal blank lines, as re-flected in Figure 3.6. Data can be entered into the blank line using the line modification procedure, given above.

The procedure to replicate a line of a report entails the following steps:

■ Display the report.

■ Move the cursor to the line to be replicated.

■ Erase that line.

■ Enter the following sequence of symbols:

▶] rX

```
.DATE 18 MAR 83  11:17:54  RID    37    18 MAR 83
.                  PERSONNEL SUMMARY
*EMPLY.   EMPLOYEE     . SOCIAL  . START.S.M.E.    .JOB.          .
* NUM .     NAME       . SEC NO  . DATE .X.S.D.DPT.CLS. SALARY   .
*=====.===============.=========.======.=.=.=.===.===.=========.
 12097 JAMES, R.C.     116472097 600510 F W A 111 053 019758.90
 37148 THOMAS, W.W.    372587148 750815 M M D 557 010 057900.00
 ]2+
 48113 WILLIAMS, T.C.  491638113 470615 M M M 111 001 131690.00
 69902 ASHEN, P.C.     658219902 551201 F M A 237 053 023614.50
 74257 CARTER, J.A.    724474257 590610 M S M 111 002 095000.00
 80392 RICHARDS, D.K.  813120392 710716 F S B 415 011 029317.75
 87613 WATSON, H.T.    885747613 830103 F S B 639 014 027500.00
                 ..... END REPORT .....
```

(a) Procedure.

```
.DATE 18 MAR 83  11:18:51  RID    37    18 MAR 83
.                  PERSONNEL SUMMARY
*EMPLY.   EMPLOYEE     . SOCIAL  . START.S.M.E.    .JOB.          .
* NUM .     NAME       . SEC NO  . DATE .X.S.D.DPT.CLS. SALARY   .
*=====.===============.=========.======.=.=.=.===.===.=========.
 12097 JAMES, R.C.     116472097 600510 F W A 111 053 019758.90
 37148 THOMAS, W.W.    372587148 750815 M M D 557 010 057900.00
 42635 BORDER, S.K.    491392635 630220 M D M 557 017 036500.00

 48113 WILLIAMS, T.C.  491638113 470615 M M M 111 001 131690.00
 69902 ASHEN, P.C.     658219902 551201 F M A 237 053 023614.50
 74257 CARTER, J.A.    724474257 590610 M S M 111 002 095000.00
 80392 RICHARDS, D.K.  813120392 710716 F S B 415 011 029317.75
 87613 WATSON, H.T.    885747613 830103 F S B 639 014 027500.00
                 ..... END REPORT .....
```

(b) Result.

Figure 3.6 Line addition.

where: ► is the Start-of-Entry character.
       ] is the right bracket.
       r is the number of times to replicate the line.
       X is the alphabetic character "X" meaning "repli-
          cate lines".

■ Transmit the entry to the computer.

```
.DATE 18 MAR 83  11:19:54  RID     37    18 MAR 83
.                   PERSONNEL SUMMARY
*EMPLY.   EMPLOYEE    . SOCIAL  . START.S.M.E.   .JOB.          .
* NUM .     NAME      . SEC NO  . DATE .X.S.D.DPT.CLS. SALARY  .
*=====.================.=========.======.=.=.=.===.===.=========.
 12097 JAMES, R.C.     116472097 600510 F W A 111 053 019758.90
 37148 THOMAS, W.W.    372587148 750815 M M D 557 010 057900.00
 ]2x3
 48113 WILLIAMS, T.C.  491638113 470615 M M M 111 001 131690.00
 69902 ASHEN, P.C.     658219902 551201 F M A 237 053 023614.50
 74257 CARTER, J.A.    724474257 590610 M S M 111 002 095000.00
 80392 RICHARDS, D.K.  813120392 710716 F S B 415 011 029317.75
 87613 WATSON, H.T.    885747613 830103 F S B 639 014 027500.00
                    ..... END REPORT .....
```

(a) Procedure.

```
.DATE 18 MAR 83  11:20:34  RID     37    18 MAR 83
.                   PERSONNEL SUMMARY
*EMPLY.   EMPLOYEE    . SOCIAL  . START.S.M.E.   .JOB.           .
* NUM .     NAME      . SEC NO  . DATE .X.S.D.DPT.CLS. SALARY   .
*=====.================.=========.======.=.=.=.===.===.=========.
 12097 JAMES, R.C.     116472097 600510 F W A 111 053 019758.90
 37148 THOMAS, W.W.    372587148 750815 M M D 557 010 057900.00
 42635 BORDER, S.K.    491392635 630220 M D M 557 017 036500.00
 48113 WILLIAMS, T.C.  491638113 470615 M M M 111 001 131690.00
 69902 ASHEN, P.C.     658219902 551201 F M A 237 053 023614.50
 42635 BORDER, S.K.    491392635 630220 M D M 557 017 036500.00
 48113 WILLIAMS, T.C.  491638113 470615 M M M 111 001 131690.00
 69902 ASHEN, P.C.     658219902 551201 F M A 237 053 023614.50
 42635 BORDER, S.K.    491392635 630220 M D M 557 017 036500.00
 48113 WILLIAMS, T.C.  491638113 470615 M M M 111 001 131690.00
 69902 ASHEN, P.C.     658219902 551201 F M A 237 053 023614.50
 74257 CARTER, J.A.    724474257 590610 M S M 111 002 095000.00
 80392 RICHARDS, D.K.  813120392 710716 F S B 415 011 029317.75
 87613 WATSON, H.T.    885747613 830103 F S B 639 014 027500.00
                    ..... END REPORT .....
```

(b) Result

Figure 3.7 Line replication.

At that point, the target line will be replicated the specified number of times, as demonstrated in Figure 3.7. This procedure is extended through an entry of the form:

▶]rXn

where r is again the number of replications, and n is the number of lines to be reproduced, as in:

▶]2X5

which indicates that two additional copies of the five lines beginning with the current cursor position should be added to the report.

The procedure for deleting lines from a report entails the following steps:

- Display the report.
- Move the cursor to the first line to be deleted.
- Erase that line.
- Enter the following sequence of symbols:

  ▶]n–

  where: ▶ is the Start-of-Entry character.
  ] is the right bracket.
  n is the number of lines to be deleted including the line at the current cursor position.
  – is a minus sign, meaning "delete lines".
- Transmit the entry to the computer.

At that point, the specified lines are deleted from the report and the free line space is closed up, as depicted in Figure 3.8.

Lines can also be adjusted within a report in either of two modes:

- Insert mode.
- Move mode.

In the *insert mode*, a copy of one or more lines is made and placed somewhere else within a report. In the *move mode*, one or more lines are literally moved from one place in a report to another. The procedure for in-

```
.DATE 18 MAR 83  11:22:48  RID     37    18 MAR 83
.                  PERSONNEL SUMMARY
*EMPLY.    EMPLOYEE  . SOCIAL  . START.S.M.E.   .JOB.          .
* NUM .      NAME    . SEC NO  . DATE .X.S.D.DPT.CLS. SALARY   .
*=====.===========.==========.=========.=====.=.=.=.===.===.=========.
 12097 JAMES, R.C.    116472097 600510 F W A 111 053 019758.90
 37148 THOMAS, W.W.   372587148 750815 M M D 557 010 057900.00
 42635 BORDER, S.K.   491392635 630220 M D M 557 017 036500.00
 48113 WILLIAMS, T.C. 491638113 470615 M M M 111 001 131690.00
 69902 ASHEN, P.C.    658219902 551201 F M A 237 053 023614.50
 ]6-
 48113 WILLIAMS, T.C. 491638113 470615 M M M 111 001 131690.00
 69902 ASHEN, P.C.    658219902 551201 F M A 237 053 023614.50
 42635 BORDER, S.K.   491392635 630220 M D M 557 017 036500.00
 48113 WILLIAMS, T.C. 491638113 470615 M M M 111 001 131690.00
 69902 ASHEN, P.C.    658219902 551201 F M A 237 053 023614.50
 74257 CARTER, J.A.   724474257 590610 M S M 111 002 095000.00
 80392 RICHARDS, D.K. 813120392 710716 F S B 415 011 029317.75
 87613 WATSON, H.T.   885747613 830103 F S B 639 014 027500.00
              ..... END REPORT .....
```

(a) Procedure.

```
.DATE 18 MAR 83  11:23:23  RID     37    18 MAR 83
.                  PERSONNEL SUMMARY
*EMPLY.    EMPLOYEE  . SOCIAL  . START.S.M.E.   .JOB.          .
* NUM .      NAME    . SEC NO  . DATE .X.S.D.DPT.CLS. SALARY   .
*=====.===========.==========.=========.=====.=.=.=.===.===.=========.
 12097 JAMES, R.C.    116472097 600510 F W A 111 053 019758.90
 37148 THOMAS, W.W.   372587148 750815 M M D 557 010 057900.00
 42635 BORDER, S.K.   491392635 630220 M D M 557 017 036500.00
 48113 WILLIAMS, T.C. 491638113 470615 M M M 111 001 131690.00
 69902 ASHEN, P.C.    658219902 551201 F M A 237 053 023614.50
 74257 CARTER, J.A.   724474257 590610 M S M 111 002 095000.00
 80392 RICHARDS, D.K. 813120392 710716 F S B 415 011 029317.75
 87613 WATSON, H.T.   885747613 830103 F S B 639 014 027500.00
              ..... END REPORT .....
```

(b) Result.

Figure 3.8 Line deletion.

serting lines in a report from another location in the same report involves the following steps:

- Display the report.
- Move the cursor to the line after which the insertion should be made.
- Erase that line.
- Enter the following sequence of symbols:

  ▶]rls,n

where: ▶ is the Start-of-Entry character.
] is the right bracket.
r is the number of times to insert the lines.
I is the alphabetic character "I" meaning "insert".
s is the starting line number.
n is the number of lines to be inserted.

■ Transmit the entry to the computer.

After the insertion function has been completed, the requested number of lines to be inserted have been placed after the cursor line. The inserted lines, i.e. the source lines, remain intact at their original location. Figure 3.9 demonstrates a line insertion operation.

```
.DATE 18 MAR 83  11:28:50  RID      37    18 MAR 83
.                   PERSONNEL SUMMARY
*EMPLY.   EMPLOYEE   . SOCIAL  . START.S.M.E.   .JOB.          .
* NUM .    NAME      . SEC NO  . DATE .X.S.D.DPT.CLS. SALARY   .
*=====.================.=========.======.=.=.=.===.===.=========.
 12097 JAMES, R.C.      116472097 600510 F W A 111 053 019758.90
 ]2i11,2
 42635 BORDER, S.K.     491392635 630220 M D M 557 017 036500.00
 48113 WILLIAMS, T.C.   491638113 470615 M M M 111 001 131690.00
 69902 ASHEN, P.C.      658219902 551201 F M A 237 053 023614.50
 74257 CARTER, J.A.     724474257 590610 M S M 111 002 095000.00
 80392 RICHARDS, D.K.   813120392 710716 F S B 415 011 029317.75
 87613 WATSON, H.T.     885747613 830103 F S B 639 014 027500.00
                  ..... END REPORT .....
```

(a) Procedure.

```
.DATE 18 MAR 83  11:29:44  RID      37    18 MAR 83
.                   PERSONNEL SUMMARY
*EMPLY.   EMPLOYEE   . SOCIAL  . START.S.M.E.   .JOB.          .
* NUM .    NAME      . SEC NO  . DATE .X.S.D.DPT.CLS. SALARY   .
*=====.================.=========.======.=.=.=.===.===.=========.
 12097 JAMES, R.C.      116472097 600510 F W A 111 053 019758.90
 37148 THOMAS, W.W.     372587148 750815 M M D 557 010 057900.00
 74257 CARTER, J.A.     724474257 590610 M S M 111 002 095000.00
 80392 RICHARDS, D.K.   813120392 710716 F S B 415 011 029317.75
 74257 CARTER, J.A.     724474257 590610 M S M 111 002 095000.00
 80392 RICHARDS, D.K.   813120392 710716 F S B 415 011 029317.75
 42635 BORDER, S.K.     491392635 630220 M D M 557 017 036500.00
 48113 WILLIAMS, T.C.   491638113 470615 M M M 111 001 131690.00
 69902 ASHEN, P.C.      658219902 551201 F M A 237 053 023614.50
 74257 CARTER, J.A.     724474257 590610 M S M 111 002 095000.00
 80392 RICHARDS, D.K.   813120392 710716 F S B 415 011 029317.75
 87613 WATSON, H.T.     885747613 830103 F S B 639 014 027500.00
                  ..... END REPORT .....
```

(b) Result.

Figure 3.9 Line insertion.

The procedure for moving lines in a report from one location to another requires the following steps:

- Display the report.

- Move the cursor to the line after which the line to be moved should be replaced.

- Erase the line.

- Enter the following sequence of symbols:

  ►] rMs,n

  where: ► is the Start-of-Entry character.

  ]   is the right bracket.

  r   is the number of lines to move the specified lines.

  M   is the alphabetic character "M" meaning "movement".

  s   is the starting line number.

  n   is the number of lines to be moved.

- Transmit the entry to the computer.

After the move line function has been completed, the moved lines have been removed from their original location as a result of the operation. Figure 3.10 depicts the line movement facilities in MAPPER.

Starting line numbers always begin with the first report line and *not* the first data line. Table 3.2 contains a summary of the line modification functions.

```
.DATE 18 MAR 83  11:30:45  RID    37    18 MAR 83
.                      PERSONNEL SUMMARY
*EMPLY.   EMPLOYEE   . SOCIAL  . START.S.M.E.   .JOB.           .
* NUM .     NAME     . SEC NO  . DATE .X.S.D.DPT.CLS. SALARY   .
*=====.===============.=========.======.=.=.=.===.===.=========.
 12097 JAMES, R.C.     116472097 600510 F W A 111 053 019758.90
 ]2m11,2
 42635 BORDER, S.K.    491392635 630220 M D M 557 017 036500.00
 48113 WILLIAMS, T.C.  491638113 470615 M M M 111 001 131690.00
 69902 ASHEN, P.C.     658219902 551201 F M A 237 053 023614.50
 74257 CARTER, J.A.    724474257 590610 M S M 111 002 095000.00
 80392 RICHARDS, D.K.  813120392 710716 F S B 415 011 029317.75
 87613 WATSON, H.T.    885747613 830103 F S B 639 014 027500.00
                      ..... END REPORT .....
```

(a) Procedure.

```
.DATE 18 MAR 83  11:31:29  RID     37    18 MAR 83
.                PERSONNEL SUMMARY
*EMPLY.    EMPLOYEE    . SOCIAL  . START.S.M.E.   .JOB.          .
* NUM .     NAME       . SEC NO  . DATE .X.S.D.DPT.CLS. SALARY   .
*=====.================.=========.======.=.=.=.===.===.=========.
 12097 JAMES, R.C.      116472097 600510 F W A 111 053 019758.90
 37148 THOMAS, W.W.     372587148 750815 M M D 557 010 057900.00
 74257 CARTER, J.A.     724474257 590610 M S M 111 002 095000.00
 80392 RICHARDS, D.K.   813120392 710716 F S B 415 011 029317.75
 74257 CARTER, J.A.     724474257 590610 M S M 111 002 095000.00
 80392 RICHARDS, D.K.   813120392 710716 F S B 415 011 029317.75
 42635 BORDER, S.K.     491392635 630220 M D M 557 017 036500.00
 48113 WILLIAMS, T.C.   491638113 470615 M M M 111 001 131690.00
 69902 ASHEN, P.C.      658219902 551201 F M A 237 053 023614.50
 87613 WATSON, H.T.     885747613 830103 F S B 639 014 027500.00
                  ..... END REPORT .....
```

(b) Result.

Figure 3.10 Line movement.

Table 3.2 Summary of Line Modification Functions

Function	Form	Example	Note
Add lines	]n+	]3+	
Delete lines	]n–	]3–	
Replicate lines	]rXn	]2X3	*
Insert lines	]rIs,n	]2I5,3	†
Move lines	]rMs,n	]2M5,3	‡

Key: n is the number of lines to be added, deleted, replicated,
     inserted, or moved

   r is the replication factor denoting how many times to
     replicate, insert, or move a set of n lines

   s is the starting line number

Note: *Means make two copies of the next three lines in-
     cluding the current cursor line.
   † Means insert lines 5 through 7 two times after the
     current cursor line
   ‡ Means move lines 5 though 7 and place them two
     times after the current cursor line

Report-Oriented Functions

Once a form type has been defined and registered in the MAPPER system, instances of that report can be created, deleted, duplicated, replaced, appended, and printed—almost at will. The most commonly used report processing functions are listed in Table 3.3, along with their respective commands and descriptions. These functions are introduced here.

The Add Report (AR) command adds an instance of a MAPPER report to the data base. To add a report, the user should enter the keyword AR in the control line and transmit it to the computer. The computer responds with the following script:

ADD REPORT

TYPE ■ ENTER FORM TYPE (A THROUGH I)

After a form type is entered and transmitted to the computer, the next available RID number in that type is assigned by the MAPPER system, and a pristine copy of the report is placed on the screen. The new RID

Table 3.3 Commonly Used Report Processing Functions

Function	Command	Description
Add Report	AR	Adds a new report to the MAPPER data base
Delete Report	DR	Deletes a report from the MAPPER data base
Duplicate Report	XR	Creates a new report by duplicating an existing report
Replace Report	REP	Replaces a specified report with the report on display
Append Report: Add on	ADON	Adds a specified report to the displayed report
Append Report: Add to	ADTO	Adds the displayed report to a specified report
Print Report	PR	Causes a report to be printed on a system printer
Access Auxiliary Devices	AUX	Can be used to have a report printed at a local device

number is placed in the date line. The data lines are blank, unless pre-defined lines are specified, and the report ends with the END REPORT line, as demonstrated in Figure 3.11. Through the various line-oriented functions covered above, data is added to a new report.

There is a fast access form of the Add Report (AR) function that reduces the requisite number of computer/user interactions. To execute an Add Report function without the interactive script, an entry of the form:

AR type

(where "type" is the type of the new report) is entered in the control line and transmitted to the computer. MAPPER responds with the result given in Figure 3.11, as in the long form. A typical fast access example of the Add Report command is:

AR B

to which MAPPER would respond with the display of a pristine report of type B and a new RID number.

```
.DATE 18 MAR 83  09:39:31  RID           18 MAR 83
.                     PERSONNEL SUMMARY
*EMPLY.    EMPLOYEE   . SOCIAL  . START.S.M.E.    .JOB.            .
* NUM .      NAME     . SEC NO  . DATE .X.S.D.DPT.CLS. SALARY  .
*=====.===============.=========.======.=.=.=.===.===.=========.



            ..... END REPORT .....
```

(a) Clean report format.

```
.DATE 18 MAR 83  13:16:24  RID      39   18 MAR 83
.                     PERSONNEL SUMMARY
*EMPLY.    EMPLOYEE   . SOCIAL  . START.S.M.E.    .JOB.            .
* NUM .      NAME     . SEC NO  . DATE .X.S.D.DPT.CLS. SALARY  .
*=====.===============.=========.======.=.=.=.===.===.=========.
 50167 DALTON, C.L.    296239072 681023 M M M 237 017 033200.00
 26410 BEAL, A.M.      470581134 770215 F S B 415 014 034900.00
 91103 APPLE, T.T.     614420823 590107 M M B 639 011 042500.00
            ..... END REPORT :.....
```

(b) New report after lines are added.

Figure 3.11 Result of the add report function.

The Delete Report (DR) command deletes a report from the MAPPER data base. The procedure for deleting a report involves the following steps:

- Display the report to be deleted.
- Enter the keyword DR in the control line and transmit it to the computer.

The computer will respond with a verification request of the form:

DELETE REPORT FROM SYSTEM

RID ▪,
TYPE ,

The proper RID number and type letter must be entered, and then MAPPER report. There is one restriction on the delete report operation. The signed-on user's identification (i.e. user-id) must match one of the user-ids in the date line, or else the report will not be deleted and the following error message will be generated:

RID TO BE DELETED MUST HAVE YOUR USER I.D.

Thus, the user deleting the report must have created the report or have been the last to update it. To verify that the report has been deleted, a display operation should be tried. If the report has in fact been deleted, the following message will be displayed:

THAT RID DOES NOT EXIST IN THE FORM TYPE

It is common to make a duplicate copy of a report prior to a big update for safekeeping; if the modifications are successful, then the old version can be deleted. As a maintenance function, out-of-date reports are periodically purged from the system.

The Duplicate Report (XR) command can be used to create a new report by duplicating an existing report or a result from an inquiry, update, or arithmetic operation. The procedure for duplicating a report involves the following steps:

- Display the report or result to be duplicated.
- Enter the keyword XR in the control line and transmit it to the computer.

The report is copied into the next available RID of the same type, and the new RID number is displayed in the date line.

The Replace Report (REP) command can be used to replace one report with another report or a result from an inquiry, update, or arithmetic operation. The character line lengths of the source and destination reports must be the same. The procedure for replacing a report requires the following steps:

- Display the replacement report or request.
- Enter the keyword REP in the control line and transmit it to the computer.

The computer will respond with the following script:

REPLACE REPORT

RID ▪ ,
TYPE   ,

After manually inserting the requested information, such as

REPLACE REPORT

RID 37 ,
TYPE B ,

the user then tranmits the entire screen to the computer. MAPPER then replaces the specified RID number, provided that the user-id of the current user matches the user-id of the user who last updated the report.

Two commands are available in MAPPER for appending one report to another, producing a combined result: add on and add to. The Add On (ADON) command appends a specified report to the displayed report and involves the following procedure:

- Display the report or result to which an "add on" should be made.
- Enter the keyword ADON in the control line and transmit it to the computer.

MAPPER responds with a function request message for the report to append, as follows:

APPEND REPORT

RID ▪ ,
TYPE   ,

After manually inserting the requested information, such as

APPEND REPORT

RID 3 ,

TYPE B,

the user transmits the entire screen to the computer, MAPPER responds by appending the data, excluding header lines, of the specified report (e.g. 3B in this case) to the end of the displayed report or result. This result can then serve as input to a following command, such as duplicate report, replace report, or any of the inquiry and update commands. Figure 3.12 demonstrates the use of the ADON command.

The Add To (ADTO) command appends a set of displayed data lines to the end of a specified report and involves the following procedure:

- Display the report or result giving the data lines to be appended to the report that will be specified.

- Enter the keyword ADTO in the control line and transmit it to the computer.

```
.                  PERSONNEL SUMMARY
*EMPLY.    EMPLOYEE  . SOCIAL  . START.S.M.E.   .JOB.            .
* NUM .      NAME    . SEC NO  . DATE .X.S.D.DPT.CLS. SALARY    .
*=====.================.=========.======.=.=.=.===.===.=========.
 12097 JAMES, R.C.    116472097 600510 F W A 111 053 019758.90
 37148 THOMAS, W.W.   372587148 750815 M M D 557 010 057900.00
 42635 BORDER, S.K.   491392635 630220 M D M 557 017 036500.00
 48113 WILLIAMS, T.C. 491638113 470615 M M M 111 001 131690.00
 69902 ASHEN, P.C.    658219902 551201 F M A 237 053 023614.50
 74257 CARTER, J.A.   724474257 590610 M S M 111 002 095000.00
 80392 RICHARDS, D.K. 813120392 710716 F S B 415 011 029317.75
 87613 WATSON, H.T.   885747613 830103 F S B 639 014 027500.00
                      ..... END REPORT .....
```

(a) Report to which an "add on" should be made.

```
.                  PERSONNEL SUMMARY
*EMPLY.    EMPLOYEE  . SOCIAL  . START.S.M.E.   .JOB.            .
* NUM .      NAME    . SEC NO  . DATE .X.S.D.DPT.CLS. SALARY    .
*=====.================.=========.======.=.=.=.===.===.=========.
 50167 DALTON, C.L.   296239072 681023 M M M 237 017 033200.00
 26410 BEAL, A.M.     470581134 770215 F S B 415 014 034900.00
 91103 APPLE, T.T.    614420823 590107 M M B 639 011 042500.00
                      ..... END REPORT .....
```

(b) Report to be appended.

```
.DATE               11:32:37  RID    37    18 MAR 83
.                   PERSONNEL SUMMARY
*EMPLY.   EMPLOYEE   . SOCIAL  . START.S.M.E.   .JOB.              .
* NUM .     NAME     . SEC NO  . DATE .X.S.D.DPT.CLS. SALARY       .
*=====.============= .========= .======.=.=.=.===.===.==========.
 12097 JAMES, R.C.    116472097 600510 F W A 111 053 019758.90
 37148 THOMAS, W.W.   372587148 750815 M M D 557 010 057900.00
 42635 BORDER, S.K.   491392635 630220 M D M 557 017 036500.00
 48113 WILLIAMS, T.C. 491638113 470615 M M M 111 001 131690.00
 69902 ASHEN, P.C.    658219902 551201 F M A 237 053 023614.50
 74257 CARTER, J.A.   724474257 590610 M S M 111 002 095000.00
 80392 RICHARDS, D.K. 813120392 710716 F S B 415 011 029317.75
 87613 WATSON, H.T.   885747613 830103 F S B 639 014 027500.00
 50167 DALTON, C.L.   296239072 681023 M M M 237 017 033200.00
 26410 BEAL, A.M.     470581134 770215 F S B 415 014 034900.00
 91103 APPLE, T.T.    614420823 590107 M M B 639 011 042500.00
                      ..... END REPORT .....
```

(c) Result.

Figure 3.12 The append report function with the ADON command.

MAPPER responds with a function request message for the report to which the data lines will be appended, as follows:

APPEND REPORT

RID ■ ,

TYPE ,

After manually inserting the requested information, such as

APPEND REPORT

RID 41 ,

TYPE B,

the user transmits the entire screen to the computer. MAPPER responds by appending the data lines, excluding header lines, to the specified report (e.g. 41B in this case). Use of the ADTO command is depicted in Figure 3.13.

There are fast access forms of both the Add On (ADON) and the Add To (ADTO) commands, delineated as follows:

Function	Command	Fast-Access Form	Procedure
Add On	ADON	ADON rt	1. Display the report to which lines should be appended.
			2. Enter ADON rt in the control line and transmit it to the computer, e.g. ADON 3B.

Function	Command	Fast-Access Form	Procedure
Add To	ADTO	ADTO rt	1. Display the data lines to be appended.
			2. Enter ADTO rt in the control line and transmit it to the computer, e.g. ADTO 2B.

```
.                   PERSONNEL SUMMARY
*EMPLY.    EMPLOYEE    . SOCIAL  . START.S.M.E.   .JOB.        .
* NUM .      NAME      . SEC NO  . DATE .X.S.D.DPT.CLS. SALARY .
*=====.===============.=========.======.=.=.=.===.===.========.
 12097 JAMES, R.C.     116472097 600510 F W A 111 053 019758.90
 37148 THOMAS, W.W.    372587148 750815 M M D 557 010 057900.00
 42635 BORDER, S.K.    491392635 630220 M D M 557 017 036500.00
 48113 WILLIAMS, T.C.  491638113 470615 M M M 111 001 131690.00
 69902 ASHEN, P.C.     658219902 551201 F M A 237 053 023614.50
 74257 CARTER, J.A.    724474257 590610 M S M 111 002 095000.00
 80392 RICHARDS, D.K.  813120392 710716 F S B 415 011 029317.75
 87613 WATSON, H.T.    885747613 830103 F S B 639 014 027500.00
                 ..... END REPORT .....
```

(a) Report to be appended.

```
.                   PERSONNEL SUMMARY
*EMPLY.    EMPLOYEE    . SOCIAL  . START.S.M.E.   .JOB.        .
* NUM .      NAME      . SEC NO  . DATE .X.S.D.DPT.CLS. SALARY .
*=====.===============.=========.======.=.=.=.===.===.========.
 50167 DALTON, C.L.    296239072 681023 M M M 237 017 033200.00
 26410 BEAL, A.M.      470581134 770215 F S B 415 014 034900.00
 91103 APPLE, T.T.     614420823 590107 M M B 639 011 042500.00
                 ..... END REPORT .....
```

(b) Report to which lines are to be appended.

```
.DATE            13:35:54  RID     41    18 MAR 83
.                   PERSONNEL SUMMARY
*EMPLY.    EMPLOYEE    . SOCIAL  . START.S.M.E.   .JOB.        .
* NUM .      NAME      . SEC NO  . DATE .X.S.D.DPT.CLS. SALARY .
*=====.===============.=========.======.=.=.=.===.===.========.
 50167 DALTON, C.L.    296239072 681023 M M M 237 017 033200.00
 26410 BEAL, A.M.      470581134 770215 F S B 415 014 034900.00
 91103 APPLE, T.T.     614420823 590107 M M B 639 011 042500.00
 12097 JAMES, R.C.     116472097 600510 F W A 111 053 019758.90
 37148 THOMAS, W.W.    372587148 750815 M M D 557 010 057900.00
 42635 BORDER, S.K.    491392635 630220 M D M 557 017 036500.00
 48113 WILLIAMS, T.C.  491638113 470615 M M M 111 001 131690.00
 69902 ASHEN, P.C.     658219902 551201 F M A 237 053 023614.50
 74257 CARTER, J.A.    724474257 590610 M S M 111 002 095000.00
 80392 RICHARDS, D.K.  813120392 710716 F S B 415 011 029317.75
 87613 WATSON, H.T.    885747613 830103 F S B 639 014 027500.00
                 ..... END REPORT .....
```

(c) Result.

Figure 3.13 The append report function with the ADTO command.

where rt is the RID number and type for the respective ADON or AD-TO command.

Two different commands can be used to print MAPPER reports:

- The PRINT command is used to have a report printed on the system printer.

- The AUX command is used to have a report printed on a local communications printer, e.g. a printer attached to a video display unit.

The AUX command has multiple uses, but only the print option is covered here.

The Print command (PR) sends MAPPER reports or results to the system printer for subsequent printing. To invoke the Print function, the user should enter the keyword PR in the control line and transmit it to the computer. MAPPER responds with the script given in Figure 3.14. After entering the requested information, the entire screen is transmitted to the computer. The specified report is queued for subsequent printing.

The Auxiliary command (AUX) can be used to direct output to devices connected to terminals. To invoke the Auxiliary function, the user should enter the keyword AUX in the control line and transmit it to the computer. MAPPER responds with the script given in Figure 3.15. After entering the requested information the entire screen is transmitted to the computer. As with the print command, the specified report is queued for subsequent printing when the device is free.

```
            MAPPER PRINT REQUEST

                 PRINT SITE ██
                   LOCATION
          NUMBER OF COPIES
              LINE SPACING
  IGNORE LINE SEQUENCE NUMBERS
          SPECIAL FORMS ID
      PRINT ALL OF A TYPE
                   FORMAT
                      RID
                     TYPE
```

Figure 3.14 Script for the Print command (PR).

```
                    AUX DEVICE REQUEST

            STATION ▓▓                    DEVICE COP
                 ID                       TAB CODES
         TRANSPARENT                   DELETE HEADERS
        LINE SPACING             DELETE 1ST CHARACTER
 DELETE LINE NUMBERS  Y                      FORMAT
                RID  -                         TYPE
```

Figure 3.15 Script for the Auxiliary command (AUX).

Summary

The effectiveness of an end-user computing system is directly related to the facilities that permit a user to access the system and generate needed results without requiring the services of a day-to-day computer specialist. A user-friendly system is needed when access is to be made by nonspecialists and occasional users. The MAPPER system is user-friendly.

The most necessary and the most basic operations in the MAPPER system are the Access and Modification functions, line-oriented functions, and report-oriented functions. The objective of the *service functions* is to get an end-user up and running as quickly as possible. The objective of the *line-oriented functions* is to allow the user to make local changes to reports. The objective of *report-oriented functions* is to manipulate reports on a global basis by dealing with a report as a unified data structure.

The service functions take good advantage of the reporting structure of the MAPPER system to assist the nonspecialist and occasional user to recall details of end-user computing. Through function (FUN) and Help (HELP) commands, the end-user has ready access to MAPPER functionality. Other commands in this class provide the capability for mode switching, displaying a report, termination and abort functions for ongoing MAPPER operations, and fast access facilities for bypassing certain levels of computer and user interaction.

The fundamental operational philosophy of the MAPPER system is that modifications can be made to reports displayed on the screen, and these changes are reflected in the underlying data structure. Because MAPPER is a total reporting system, updates are not made in place, but are postponed until a periodic reconciliation and consolidation of accumulated data base changes. The key characteristic of MAPPER operations is that visual programming enhances the level of computer/user interaction.

Most line-oriented functions are visually-oriented operations wherein a report is displayed on the screen and MAPPER functions are applied to it. The most widely-used line-oriented functions are:

- Field and line changes.
- Repaint the screen.
- Adding lines to a report.
- Replicating lines of a report.
- Deleting lines from a report.
- Inserting lines in a report.
- Moving lines in a report.

Line-oriented functions pertain to operations within the structure of a single report.

Once the type of a report has been defined and registered in the MAP-PER system, instances of that report can be created, deleted, duplicated, replaced, appended, and printed by simply regarding a report as a unified data structure. The most widely used report-oriented functions in MAP-PER are:

Function	Command
Add Report	AR
Delete Report	DR
Duplicate Report	XR
Replace Report	REP
Append Report:	
Add on	ADON
Add to	ADTO
Print Report	
System Printer	PR
Auxiliary Printer	AUX

Nearly all report-oriented functions have a fast access counterpart for speedy access to the MAPPER database.

CHAPTER FOUR

Inquiry and Update Functions

Many functions in data processing deal with a complete data structure, such as a report or a list. Typical examples are sort, search, and locate. In the MAPPER system, most data processing functions can be performed with a single command together with a mask for entering parameters needed for that particular function. This is visual programming at the textual level. This section covers a subset of the inquiry and update functions that can be entered manually from the keyboard. Moreover, the options to some of the commands are, in themselves, reasonably extensive so that the subject matter covers the most widely used options.

Introduction

In data processing, visual programming normally refers to two conditions: the capability of looking at a complete data structure, and a method of specifying options and parameters in relation to the associated data structure.

The first condition is satisfied by the facilities in MAPPER to display a report, and then to shift and scroll through that report in a convenient manner. The second condition is satisfied through a mask that permits the user to specify the fields that participate in a function and to indicate how they should be used. These concepts are conveniently demonstrated by an example.

Figure 4.1 gives an instance of the sort function, which is described in detail in a later section. The function is initiated by displaying the report to be sorted, as shown in Figure 4.1(a). The SORT command is entered in the control line and transmitted to the computer. The MAPPER system responds with the sort mask, given in Figure 4.1(b). In the mask, the column headings are given, and the asterisk fields signify possible options and parameters. In this example, a "1" is entered in the EMPLY NUM field to specify that it is the primary sort key: ascending sorted order is assumed. After the entire screen, including the mask, is transmitted to the computer, the MAPPER system responds with the results, sorted by the EMPLY NUM field and displayed in Figure 4.1(c). The key point is that the end-user can operate visually, yet achieve the same results as if a complex programming language were used.

Table 4.1 gives a representative list of MAPPER functions that can be executed manually. The list is representative because MAPPER is a continuously evolving system, and functions are normally added on a continuing basis.

Most MAPPER commands that can be entered manually have a fast access equivalent. This option is not covered further.

```
.DATE              13:33:30  RID     40     18 MAR 83
.                  PERSONNEL SUMMARY
*EMPLY.    EMPLOYEE     . SOCIAL  . START.S.M.E.   .JOB.          .
* NUM .      NAME       . SEC NO  . DATE .X.S.D.DPT.CLS. SALARY   .
*=====.===============. =========.======.=.=.=.===.===.=========.
 12097 JAMES, R.C.      116472097 600510 F W A 111 053 019758.90
 37148 THOMAS, W.W.     372587148 750815 M M D 557 010 057900.00
 42635 BORDER, S.K.     491392635 630220 M D M 557 017 036500.00
 48113 WILLIAMS, T.C.   491638113 470615 M M M 111 001 131690.00
 69902 ASHEN, P.C.      658219902 551201 F M A 237 053 023614.50
 74257 CARTER, J.A.     724474257 590610 M S M 111 002 095000.00
 80392 RICHARDS, D.K.   813120392 710716 F S B 415 011 029317.75
 87613 WATSON, H.T.     885747613 830103 F S B 639 014 027500.00
 50167 DALTON, C.L.     296239072 681023 M M M 237 017 033200.00
 26410 BEAL, A.M.       470581134 770215 F S B 415 014 034900.00
 91103 APPLE, T.T.      614420823 590107 M M B 639 011 042500.00
                       ..... END REPORT .....
```

(a) Report to be sorted.

```
.                  PERSONNEL SUMMARY
*EMPLY.    EMPLOYEE     . SOCIAL  . START.S.M.E.   .JOB.          .
* NUM .      NAME       . SEC NO  . DATE .X.S.D.DPT.CLS. SALARY   .
*=====.===============. =========.======.=.=.=.===.===.=========.
 ***** *************** ********* ****** * * * *** *** *********
 1
```

(b) Sort mask.

```
.DATE                14:14:58  RID    40    18 MAR 83
.                     PERSONNEL SUMMARY
*EMPLY.    EMPLOYEE     . SOCIAL  . START.S.M.E.    .JOB.           .
* NUM .      NAME       . SEC NO  . DATE .X.S.D.DPT.CLS. SALARY     .
*=====.================.=========.======.=.=.=.===.===.==========.
 12097 JAMES, R.C.       116472097 600510 F W A 111 053 019758.90
 26410 BEAL, A.M.        470581134 770215 F S B 415 014 034900.00
 37148 THOMAS, W.W.      372587148 750815 M M D 557 010 057900.00
 42635 BORDER, S.K.      491392635 630220 M D M 557 017 036500.00
 48113 WILLIAMS, T.C.    491638113 470615 M M M 111 001 131690.00
 50167 DALTON, C.L.      296239072 681023 M M M 237 017 033200.00
 69902 ASHEN, P.C.       658219902 551201 F M A 237 053 023614.50
 74257 CARTER, J.A.      724474257 590610 M S M 111 002 095000.00
 80392 RICHARDS, D.K.    813120392 710716 F S B 415 011 029317.75
 87613 WATSON, H.T.      885747613 830103 F S B 639 014 027500.00
 91103 APPLE, T.T.       614420823 590107 M M B 639 011 042500.00
                     ..... END REPORT .....
```

(c) Result sorted by the EMPLY NUM field.

Figure 4.1 An example of visual programming using a function mask to specify options and parameters.

Table 4.1 Representative List of MAPPER Commands That Can Be Executed Manually

Command	Function
ADON	Add on*
AR	Add report*
ADTO	Add to*
A	Arithmetic‡
AUX	Auxiliary*
START	Batch start
BF	Binary find†
CHG	Change†
COPY	Copy
DATE	Date
DR	Delete report*
DLL	Down line load
XR	Duplicate report*
ELT	Element

Table 4.1 continued

Command	Function
ELT–	Element delete
F	Find†
I	Index
LZ	Line zero
LOC	Locate†
MA	Match†
MAU	Match update
PSW	Password
PR	Print*
PUNCH	Punch cards
RF	Reformat
RR	Remote run
REP	Replace report*
RSM	Resume
RETR	Retrieve
RSI	Remote symbiont interface
S	Search†
SL	Search list
SLU	Search list update
SU	Search update
SEND	Send report
SORT	Sort report†
SS	Station-to-station message
TCS	Tape cassette
TOT	Totalize‡

Note: *Covered in chapter 3.
†Covered in this chapter.
‡Covered in chapter 5.

The Find Function

In a lengthy or complex report, it is cumbersome to visually search for the first data line that meets a given condition. Finding subsequent lines can be equally tedious. The *Find function* searches for the first occurrence of specified data in a report or form type. RIDs can be chained so that after one report has been searched, a succeeding one is referenced.

The Find function is display-oriented in the sense that the operation finds the first occurrence of a data line meeting specified criteria, and places it as the first data line on the screen. Effectively, this is a scrolling operation, since from that line, the report can be ROLLed either up or down.

To invoke the Find function, the user enters the keyword F in the control line and transmits it to the computer. The MAPPER system responds with the following script:

```
FIND REPORT DATA
     RID ■        ,
     TYPE         ,
     FORMAT       ,
```

After supplying the requested information, the entire screen is transmitted to the computer, and the MAPPER system responds with a function mask, similar to the one given previously with the sort example. After providing the requested condition, which may involve more than one field, the entire function mask screen is transmitted to the computer. MAPPER then displays the referenced report, with the first line meeting the specified conditions in the first data line position on the screen. If an entire form type is to be searched, then the RID field of the above script should be left blank. If a previous result should be searched, then a minus sign (–) should be placed in the RID field.

Figure 4.2 demonstrates the Find function for the first employee in department 237. Figure 4.2(a) gives the report to be searched and displayed. Figure 4.2(b) depicts the function mask, and Figure 4.2(c) gives the result of the Find function, which lists an employee with department number 237 in the first report line.

By entering the keyword RSM (for resume) in the control line and transmitting it to the computer, the user can request a search for another line that meets the specified condition. However, the resume for the Find

```
.DATE               14:14:58  RID     40    18 MAR 83
.                     PERSONNEL SUMMARY
*EMPLY.    EMPLOYEE    . SOCIAL   . START.S.M.E.  .JOB.           .
* NUM .     NAME       . SEC NO   . DATE .X.S.D.DPT.CLS. SALARY   .
*=====.================.==========.======.=.=.=.===.===.==========.
 12097 JAMES, R.C.      116472097 600510 F W A 111 053 019758.90
 26410 BEAL, A.M.       470581134 770215 F S B 415 014 034900.00
 37148 THOMAS, W.W.     372587148 750815 M M D 557 010 057900.00
 42635 BORDER, S.K.     491392635 630220 M D M 557 017 036500.00
 48113 WILLIAMS, T.C.   491638113 470615 M M M 111 001 131690.00
 50167 DALTON, C.L.     296239072 681023 M M M 237 017 033200.00
 69902 ASHEN, P.C.      658219902 551201 F M A 237 053 023614.50
 74257 CARTER, J.A.     724474257 590610 M S M 111 002 095000.00
 80392 RICHARDS, D.K.   813120392 710716 F S B 415 011 029317.75
 87613 WATSON, H.T.     885747613 830103 F S B 639 014 027500.00
 91103 APPLE, T.T.      614420823 590107 M M B 639 011 042500.00
                   ..... END REPORT .....
```

(a) Report to which the Find function should be applied.

```
.                     PERSONNEL SUMMARY
*EMPLY.    EMPLOYEE    . SOCIAL   . START.S.M.E.  .JOB.           .
* NUM .     NAME       . SEC NO   . DATE .X.S.D.DPT.CLS. SALARY   .
*=====.================.==========.======.=.=.=.===.===.==========.
 ***** *************** ********* ****** * * * *** *** *********
                                               237
```

(b) Find function mask.

```
LINE  11    FMT    RL  -      SHFT      HLD CHRS      HLD LN          fcs
 50167 DALTON, C.L.    296239072 681023 M M M 237 017 033200.00
 69902 ASHEN, P.C.     658219902 551201 F M A 237 053 023614.50
 74257 CARTER, J.A.    724474257 590610 M S M 111 002 095000.00
 80392 RICHARDS, D.K.  813120392 710716 F S B 415 011 029317.75
 87613 WATSON, H.T.    885747613 830103 F S B 639 014 027500.00
 91103 APPLE, T.T.     614420823 590107 M M B 639 011 042500.00
                  ..... END REPORT .....
```

(c) Result of the Find function.

Figure 4.2 Example of the Find function.

---

function works in a characteristic manner. When resume is invoked, the
MAPPER system looks for the next line that meets the given conditions
on the next screen. Thus, an implicit assumption is made that pertinent
lines already on the current screen have been identified.

The Search Function

The *Search function* scans an entire report or form type for "all" lines
that satisfy a specified condition and produces a result, i.e. a report containing only those lines. The Search function is invoked by entering the

keyword S in the control line and transmitting it to the computer. The MAPPER system responds with the following script:

                    SEARCH REPORT DATA
                         RID   ■   ,
                         TYPE   ,
                         FORMAT   ,

After supplying the requested information, the entire screen is transmitted to the computer, and the MAPPER system responds with a function mask. After specifying a condition, which can take one of several forms ranging from simple to complex, the entire function mask screen is transmitted to the computer. The MAPPER system then selects lines from the reference report, creates a "results" report, and displays it. Figure 4.3 gives an example of a simple search operation for all personnel in department 111. The result gives the ordinal number of lines that satisfied the specified condition, a copy of the mask, and a display of the result. Whereas the Find function displays only the first, or subsequent, occurrence of a given condition, the Search function displays all occurrences.

As with the Find function, the Search command can be used to scan a single report or an entire form type. In the latter case, the RID field must be left blank in the above script. If a result report is to be searched, then a minus RID must be given.

There are at least 15 additional options to the Search function that provide alternatives such as range searching and inverse searching. One of the most frequently used options is range searching, which is covered here.

```
.DATE              14:14:58  RID    40    18 MAR 83
.                     PERSONNEL SUMMARY
*EMPLY.   EMPLOYEE     . SOCIAL  . START.S.M.E.   .JOB.          .
* NUM .    NAME        . SEC NO  . DATE .X.S.D.DPT.CLS. SALARY  .
*=====.=================.=========.======.=.=.=.===.===.=========.
 12097 JAMES, R.C.      116472097 600510 F W A 111 053 019758.90
 26410 BEAL, A.M.       470581134 770215 F S B 415 014 034900.00
 37148 THOMAS, W.W.     372587148 750815 M M D 557 010 057900.00
 42635 BORDER, S.K.     491392635 630220 M D M 557 017 036500.00
 48113 WILLIAMS, T.C.   491638113 470615 M M M 111 001 131690.00
 50167 DALTON, C.L.     296239072 681023 M M M 237 017 033200.00
 69902 ASHEN, P.C.      658219902 551201 F M A 237 053 023614.50
 74257 CARTER, J.A.     724474257 590610 M S M 111 002 095000.00
 80392 RICHARDS, D.K.   813120392 710716 F S B 415 011 029317.75
 87613 WATSON, H.T.     885747613 830103 F S B 639 014 027500.00
 91103 APPLE, T.T.      614420823 590107 M M B 639 011 042500.00
                    ..... END REPORT .....
```

(a) Report to which the Search function should be applied.

```
.                    PERSONNEL SUMMARY
*EMPLY.   EMPLOYEE   . SOCIAL   . START.S.M.E.   .JOB.        .
* NUM .     NAME     . SEC NO   . DATE .X.S.D.DPT.CLS. SALARY .
*=====.===============.=========.======.=.=.=.===.===.=========.
 ***** *************** ********* ****** * * * *** *** *********
                                                      111
```

(b) Search function mask.

```
.
.      3 LINES FOUND OUT OF  11 LINES
..
****** *************** ********* ****** * * * *** *** *********
*                                                     111
. .  .
.DATE              14:14:58  RID    40     18 MAR 83
.                    PERSONNEL SUMMARY
*EMPLY.   EMPLOYEE   . SOCIAL   . START.S.M.E.   .JOB.        .
* NUM .     NAME     . SEC NO   . DATE .X.S.D.DPT.CLS. SALARY .
*=====.===============.=========.======.=.=.=.===.===.=========.
 12097 JAMES, R.C.    116472097 600510 F W A 111 053 019758.90
 48113 WILLIAMS, T.C. 491638113 470615 M M M 111 001 131690.00
 74257 CARTER, J.A.   724474257 590610 M S M 111 002 095000.00
                      ..... END REPORT .....
```

(c) Result of the Search function.

Figure 4.3 Example of a single Search function.

```
.DATE              14:14:58  RID    40     18 MAR 83
.                    PERSONNEL SUMMARY
*EMPLY.   EMPLOYEE   . SOCIAL   . START.S.M.E.   .JOB.        .
* NUM .     NAME     . SEC NO   . DATE .X.S.D.DPT.CLS. SALARY .
*=====.===============.=========.======.=.=.=.===.===.=========.
 12097 JAMES, R.C.    116472097 600510 F W A 111 053 019758.90
 26410 BEAL, A.M.     470581134 770215 F S B 415 014 034900.00
 37148 THOMAS, W.W.   372587148 750815 M M D 557 010 057900.00
 42635 BORDER, S.K.   491392635 630220 M D M 557 017 036500.00
 48113 WILLIAMS, T.C. 491638113 470615 M M M 111 001 131690.00
 50167 DALTON, C.L.   296239072 681023 M M M 237 017 033200.00
 69902 ASHEN, P.C.    658219902 551201 F M A 237 053 023614.50
 74257 CARTER, J.A.   724474257 590610 M S M 111 002 095000.00
 80392 RICHARDS, D.K. 813120392 710716 F S B 415 011 029317.75
 87613 WATSON, H.T.   885747613 830103 F S B 639 014 027500.00
 91103 APPLE, T.T.    614420823 590107 M M B 639 011 042500.00
                      ..... END REPORT .....
```

(a) Report to which the range search function should be applied.

```
.                    PERSONNEL SUMMARY
*EMPLY.   EMPLOYEE   . SOCIAL   . START.S.M.E.   .JOB.        .
* NUM .     NAME     . SEC NO   . DATE .X.S.D.DPT.CLS. SALARY .
*=====.===============.=========.======.=.=.=.===.===.=========.
 ***** *************** ********* ****** * * * *** *** *********
                                                      040000.00
 r                                                    999999.99
```

(b) Range search function mask.

```
  .
  .     4 LINES FOUND OUT OF 11 LINES
  .
  .****** *************** ********* ****** * * * *** *** *********
  *                                                    040000.00
  .THRU
  *                                                    999999.99
  .   .   .
  .DATE            14:14:58  RID      40     18 MAR 83
  .                        PERSONNEL SUMMARY
  *EMPLY.   EMPLOYEE    . SOCIAL  . START.S.M.E.    .JOB.         .
  * NUM .     NAME      . SEC NO  . DATE .X.S.D.DPT.CLS. SALARY   .
  *=====. ===============. =========. ======.=.=.=.===.===.=========.
   37148 THOMAS, W.W.    372587148 750815 M M D 557 010 057900.00
   48113 WILLIAMS, T.C.  491638113 470615 M M M 111 001 131690.00
   74257 CARTER, J.A.    724474257 590610 M S M 111 002 095000.00
   91103 APPLE, T.T.     614420823 590107 M M B 639 011 042500.00
                         ..... END REPORT .....
```

(c) Result of the range search function.

Figure 4.4 Example of a range search function.

In the personnel summary report, suppose that it is necessary to search for all employees making $40,000 or higher salary. This example is shown in Figure 4.4. The original report and the result are straightforward. The Search function mask denotes a range by the salary value of 040000.00 in line 1 and the value of 999999.99 in line 2. The character "r" must be in column 1 of the second line to specify a range. The range search is also denoted in the result where the character "r" is replaced by the key-word THRU.

Because the Search function generates a "result" report, the user may perform any MAPPER function on it, such as scrolling, replace report, or print report.

The Locate Function

Most MAPPER functions perform column-dependent operations, and the Find and Search functions are good instances of this fact. The Locate function is one of several exceptions.

The *Locate function* performs a column-independent scan of a report; it is conceptually similar to the Find function. The Locate function locates the first occurrence of a data line meeting specified column-independent conditions, and places it as the first data line on the screen. This is also a scrolling operation, as with the Find function, so that the report can be ROLLed up or down after the Locate function has been executed. The Locate function does not generate a new report as a result.

To invoke the Locate function, the user enters the keyword LOC in the control line and transmits it to the computer. The MAPPER system responds with a script, requesting the RID, TYPE, and FORMAT for the object report. This facility is identical to the script for the Find and Search functions. After the scope of the Locate function has been entered, the MAPPER system responds with the usual function mask. Figure 4.5 gives an example of the Locate function to show how the function mask works in this instance. The character string to be located in the report is placed on the first line under the mask starting in column

```
.DATE           14:14:58  RID      40    18 MAR 83
.                    PERSONNEL SUMMARY
*EMPLY.    EMPLOYEE  . SOCIAL  . START.S.M.E.    .JOB.          .
* NUM .      NAME    . SEC NO  . DATE .X.S.D.DPT.CLS. SALARY    .
*=====. ================. =========. ======.=.=.=. ===. ===. =========.
 12097 JAMES, R.C.      116472097 600510 F W A 111 053 019758.90
 26410 BEAL, A.M.       470581134 770215 F S B 415 014 034900.00
 37148 THOMAS, W.W.     372587148 750815 M M D 557 010 057900.00
 42635 BORDER, S.K.     491392635 630220 M D M 557 017 036500.00
 48113 WILLIAMS, T.C.   491638113 470615 M M M 111 001 131690.00
 50167 DALTON, C.L.     296239072 681023 M M M 237 017 033200.00
 69902 ASHEN, P.C.      658219902 551201 F M A 237 053 023614.50
 74257 CARTER, J.A.     724474257 590610 M S M 111 002 095000.00
 80392 RICHARDS, D.K.   813120392 710716 F S B 415 011 029317.75
 87613 WATSON, H.T.     885747613 830103 F S B 639 014 027500.00
 91103 APPLE, T.T.      614420823 590107 M M B 639 011 042500.00
                     ..... END REPORT .....
```

(a) Report to which the Locate function is applied.

```
.                    PERSONNEL SUMMARY
*EMPLY.    EMPLOYEE  . SOCIAL  . START.S.M.E.    .JOB.          .
* NUM .      NAME    . SEC NO  . DATE .X.S.D.DPT.CLS. SALARY    .
*=====. ================. =========. ======.=.=.=. ===. ===. =========.
***** *************** ********* ****** * * * *** *** *********
 CARTER
```

(b) Locate function mask.

```
LINE  13    FMT    RL -     SHFT     HLD CHRS     HLD LN    fcs
 74257 CARTER, J.A.     724474257 590610 M S M 111 002 095000.00
 80392 RICHARDS, D.K.   813120392 710716 F S B 415 011 029317.75
 87613 WATSON, H.T.     885747613 830103 F S B 639 014 027500.00
 91103 APPLE, T.T.      614420823 590107 M M B 639 011 042500.00
                     ..... END REPORT .....
```

(c) Result of the Locate function.

Figure 4.5 Example of the Locate function.

1, as is the case with the word CARTER in Figure 4.5(b). The MAPPER system locates the first instance of the specified character string.

The Locate function can be resumed by entering the keyword RSM in the control line and transmitting it to the computer. The scan halts with the very next occurrence of the specified string in a data line, unlike the Find function.

The Sort Function

The *Sort function* can be used to reorder lines in a report or in a result on display. Figure 4.1, covered earlier, contains an example of a single-level ascending sort. A single-level sort is a reordering based on a single field; a multi-level sort is a reordering based on multiple fields. A sort may be based on ascending values, descending values, or a combination of ascending and descending values.

Figure 4.6 gives an example of an ascending alphabetic sort, wherein a report is sorted by the EMPLOYEE NAME field. The sort operations demonstrated in Figures 4.1 and 4.6 both reflect alphabetic sorts based

```
.DATE              14:14:58  RID      40     18 MAR 83
.                    PERSONNEL SUMMARY
*EMPLY.   EMPLOYEE    . SOCIAL   . START.S.M.E.    .JOB.            .
* NUM .     NAME      . SEC NO   . DATE .X.S.D.DPT.CLS. SALARY    .
*=====.================.=========.======.=.=.=.===.===.=========.
 12097 JAMES, R.C.     116472097 600510 F W A 111 053 019758.90
 26410 BEAL, A.M.      470581134 770215 F S B 415 014 034900.00
 37148 THOMAS, W.W.    372587148 750815 M M D 557 010 057900.00
 42635 BORDER, S.K.    491392635 630220 M D M 557 017 036500.00
 48113 WILLIAMS, T.C.  491638113 470615 M M M 111 001 131690.00
 50167 DALTON, C.L.    296239072 681023 M M M 237 017 033200.00
 69902 ASHEN, P.C.     658219902 551201 F M A 237 053 023614.50
 74257 CARTER, J.A.    724474257 590610 M S M 111 002 095000.00
 80392 RICHARDS, D.K.  813120392 710716 F S B 415 011 029317.75
 87613 WATSON, H.T.    885747613 830103 F S B 639 014 027500.00
 91103 APPLE, T.T.     614420823 590107 M M B 639 011 042500.00
                       ..... END REPORT .....
```

(a) Report to be sorted.

```
.                    PERSONNEL SUMMARY
*EMPLY.   EMPLOYEE    . SOCIAL   . START.S.M.E.    .JOB.            .
* NUM .     NAME      . SEC NO   . DATE .X.S.D.DPT.CLS. SALARY    .
*=====.================.=========.======.=.=.=.===.===.=========.
 ***** *************** ********* ****** * * * *** *** *********
       1
```

(b) Sort mask.

```
.DATE                14:14:58  RID     40    18 MAR 83
.                       PERSONNEL SUMMARY
*EMPLY.    EMPLOYEE      . SOCIAL   . START.S.M.E.    .JOB.          .
* NUM .      NAME        . SEC NO   . DATE .X.S.D.DPT.CLS. SALARY    .
*=====.================.==========.======.=.=.=.===.===.=========.
  91103 APPLE,  T.T.      614420823 590107 M M B 639 011 042500.00
  69902 ASHEN,  P.C.      658219902 551201 F M A 237 053 023614.50
  26410 BEAL,  A.M.       470581134 770215 F S B 415 014 034900.00
  42635 BORDER,  S.K.     491392635 630220 M D M 557 017 036500.00
  74257 CARTER,  J.A.     724474257 590610 M S M 111 002 095000.00
  50167 DALTON,  C.L.     296239072 681023 M M M 237 017 033200.00
  12097 JAMES,  R.C.      116472097 600510 F W A 111 053 019758.90
  80392 RICHARDS,  D.K.   813120392 710716 F S B 415 011 029317.75
  37148 THOMAS,  W.W.     372587148 750815 M M D 557 010 057900.00
  87613 WATSON,  H.T.     885747613 830103 F S B 639 014 027500.00
  48113 WILLIAMS,  T.C.   491638113 470615 M M M 111 001 131690.00
                        ..... END REPORT .....
```

(c) Result sorted by EMPLOYEE NAME field.

Figure 4.6 Example of the Sort function.

on the collating sequence of the underlying character set. It is immaterial whether the characters sorted are alphabetic characters or numeric characters. Special procedures are available in MAPPER for sorting on the algebraic contents of a field.

Figure 4.7 gives an example of a multi-level ascending sort based first on the field DPT then on START DATE. The number 1 in the function

```
.DATE                14:14:58  RID     40    18 MAR 83
.                       PERSONNEL SUMMARY
*EMPLY.    EMPLOYEE      . SOCIAL   . START.S.M.E.    .JOB.          .
* NUM .      NAME        . SEC NO   . DATE .X.S.D.DPT.CLS. SALARY    .
*=====.================.==========.======.=.=.=.===.===.=========.
  12097 JAMES,  R.C.      116472097 600510 F W A 111 053 019758.90
  26410 BEAL,  A.M.       470581134 770215 F S B 415 014 034900.00
  37148 THOMAS,  W.W.     372587148 750815 M M D 557 010 057900.00
  42635 BORDER,  S.K.     491392635 630220 M D M 557 017 036500.00
  48113 WILLIAMS,  T.C.   491638113 470615 M M M 111 001 131690.00
  50167 DALTON,  C.L.     296239072 681023 M M M 237 017 033200.00
  69902 ASHEN,  P.C.      658219902 551201 F M A 237 053 023614.50
  74257 CARTER,  J.A.     724474257 590610 M S M 111 002 095000.00
  80392 RICHARDS,  D.K.   813120392 710716 F S B 415 011 029317.75
  87613 WATSON,  H.T.     885747613 830103 F S B 639 014 027500.00
  91103 APPLE,  T.T.      614420823 590107 M M B 639 011 042500.00
                        ..... END REPORT .....
```

(a) Report to be sorted.

```
.                       PERSONNEL SUMMARY
*EMPLY.    EMPLOYEE      . SOCIAL   . START.S.M.E.    .JOB.          .
* NUM .      NAME        . SEC NO   . DATE .X.S.D.DPT.CLS. SALARY    .
*=====.================.==========.======.=.=.=.===.===.=========.
 ***** **************** ********* ****** * * * *** *** *********
                          2                 1
```

(b) Multi-level sort mask.

```
. DATE              14:14:58  RID     40    18 MAR 83
.                      PERSONNEL SUMMARY
*EMPLY.   EMPLOYEE   . SOCIAL  . START.S.M.E.   .JOB.          .
* NUM .     NAME     . SEC NO  . DATE .X.S.D.DPT.CLS. SALARY   .
*=====.=============.=========.======.=.=.=.===.===.=========.
 48113 WILLIAMS, T.C. 491638113 470615 M M M 111 001 131690.00
 74257 CARTER, J.A.   724474257 590610 M S M 111 002 095000.00
 12097 JAMES, R.C.    116472097 600510 F W A 111 053 019758.90
 69902 ASHEN, P.C.    658219902 551201 F M A 237 053 023614.50
 50167 DALTON, C.L.   296239072 681023 M M M 237 017 033200.00
 80392 RICHARDS, D.K. 813120392 710716 F S B 415 011 029317.75
 26410 BEAL, A.M.     470581134 770215 F S B 415 014 034900.00
 42635 BORDER, S.K.   491392635 630220 M D M 557 017 036500.00
 37148 THOMAS, W.W.   372587148 750815 M M D 557 010 057900.00
 91103 APPLE, T.T.    614420823 590107 M M B 639 011 042500.00
 87613 WATSON, H.T.   885747613 830103 F S B 639 014 027500.00
                      ..... END REPORT .....
```

(c) Result of the multi-level sort.

Figure 4.7 Example of a multi-level sort mask.

mask denotes the primary key; the number 2 denotes the secondary key; and so forth.

Table 4.2 gives a representative set of sort specifications based on ascending and descending modalities. A descending specification is denoted by the letter "d" following the key indicator. A numeric sort based on algebraic values is specified by the letter "n". The numeric sort is always in ascending order with the smallest algebraic value first.

Table 4.2 Sort Specifications

Sort Function Mask			Sort Specifications
*FIELD A	. FIELD B	. FIELD C .	
*=======	. =======	. ======= .	
*******	*******	*******	
	1		Single level-ascending
		1d	Single level-descending
2	1		Multi-level-ascending
	1d	2d	Multi-level-descending
	2d	1	Multi-level-ascending and descending
1n			Single level-numeric

The Binary Find Function

Most persons in data processing are familiar with a binary search, wherein a sorted search key is sampled at interval midpoints to reduce search time. The Binary Find function applies the same logic to the MAPPER Find function. The actual execution of the Binary Find function involves the use of an index to facilitate the find operation.

In its most simple form, the Binary Find function operates in exactly the same manner as the Find function, covered previously. The major difference is that the function mask specification must indicate a sorted field, as demonstrated in the example given in Figure 4.8. The Binary Find function is particularly efficient for large-sized RIDs.

```
.DATE            09:10:47  RID    40    23 MAR 83
.                 PERSONNEL SUMMARY
*EMPLY.   EMPLOYEE   . SOCIAL  . START.S.M.E.   .JOB.           .
* NUM .     NAME     . SEC NO  . DATE .X.S.D.DPT.CLS. SALARY    .
*=====.=============.=========.======.=.=.=.===.===.=========.
 48113 WILLIAMS, T.C. 491638113 470615 M M M 111 001 131690.00
 74257 CARTER, J.A.   724474257 590610 M S M 111 002 095000.00
 12097 JAMES, R.C.    116472097 600510 F W A 111 053 019758.90
 69902 ASHEN, P.C.    658219902 551201 F M A 237 053 023614.50
 50167 DALTON, C.L.   296239072 681023 M M M 237 017 033200.00
 80392 RICHARDS, D.K. 813120392 710716 F S B 415 011 029317.75
 26410 BEAL, A.M.     470581134 770215 F S B 415 014 034900.00
 42635 BORDER, S.K.   491392635 630220 M D M 557 017 036500.00
 37148 THOMAS, W.W.   372587148 750815 M M D 557 010 057900.00
 91103 APPLE, T.T.    614420823 590107 M M B 639 011 042500.00
 87613 WATSON, H.T.   885747613 830103 F S B 639 014 027500.00
                      ..... END REPORT .....
```

(a) Report to which the Binary Find function is to be applied.

```
.                 PERSONNEL SUMMARY
*EMPLY.   EMPLOYEE   . SOCIAL  . START.S.M.E.   .JOB.           .
* NUM .     NAME     . SEC NO  . DATE .X.S.D.DPT.CLS. SALARY    .
*=====.=============.=========.======.=.=.=.===.===.=========.
***** ************** ********* ****** * * * *** *** *********
                                              415
```

(b) Function mask indicating a sorted field.

```
LINE  11    FMT    RL   -      SHFT      HLD CHRS     HLD LN
 80392 RICHARDS, D.K. 813120392 710716 F S B 415 011 029317.75
 26410 BEAL, A.M.     470581134 770215 F S B 415 014 034900.00
 42635 BORDER, S.K.   491392635 630220 M D M 557 017 036500.00
 37148 THOMAS, W.W.   372587148 750815 M M D 557 010 057900.00
 91103 APPLE, T.T.    614420823 590107 M M B 639 011 042500.00
 87613 WATSON, H.T.   885747613 830103 F S B 639 014 027500.00
                      ..... END REPORT .....
```

(c) Result of the Binary Find function.

Figure 4.8 Simple case of the Binary Find function.

```
.DATE                09:10:47  RID      40     23 MAR 83
.                       PERSONNEL SUMMARY
*EMPLY.     EMPLOYEE    . SOCIAL   . START.S.M.E.    .JOB.          .
* NUM .       NAME      . SEC NO   . DATE .X.S.D.DPT.CLS. SALARY    .
*=====.================.=========.======.=.=.=.===.===.=========.
 48113 WILLIAMS, T.C.   491638113 470615 M M M 111 001 131690.00
 74257 CARTER, J.A.     724474257 590610 M S M 111 002 095000.00
 12097 JAMES, R.C.      116472097 600510 F W A 111 053 019758.90
 69902 ASHEN, P.C.      658219902 551201 F M A 237 053 023614.50
 50167 DALTON, C.L.     296239072 681023 M M M 237 017 033200.00
 80392 RICHARDS, D.K.   813120392 710716 F S B 415 011 029317.75
 26410 BEAL, A.M.       470581134 770215 F S B 415 014 034900.00
 42635 BORDER, S.K.     491392635 630220 M D M 557 017 036500.00
 37148 THOMAS, W.W.     372587148 750815 M M D 557 010 057900.00
 91103 APPLE, T.T.      614420823 590107 M M B 639 011 042500.00
 87613 WATSON, H.T.     885747613 830103 F S B 639 014 027500.00
                        ..... END REPORT .....
```

(a) Report to which the Binary Find N option is to be applied.

```
n
.                       PERSONNEL SUMMARY
*EMPLY.     EMPLOYEE    . SOCIAL   . START.S.M.E.    .JOB.          .
* NUM .       NAME      . SEC NO   . DATE .X.S.D.DPT.CLS. SALARY    .
*=====.================.=========.======.=.=.=.===.===.=========.
 ***** **************** ********* ****** * * * *** *** *********
                                                 k    =
```

(b) Function mask indicating the N option, the field to be counted (k),
    and the field to place the count (denoted by =).

```
.DATE                09:10:47  RID      40     23 MAR 83
.                       PERSONNEL SUMMARY
*EMPLY.     EMPLOYEE    . SOCIAL   . START.S.M.E.    .JOB.          .
* NUM .       NAME      . SEC NO   . DATE .X.S.D.DPT.CLS. SALARY    .
*=====.================.=========.======.=.=.=.===.===.=========.
 12097 JAMES, R.C.      116472097 600510 F W A 111   3 019758.90
 50167 DALTON, C.L.     296239072 681023 M M M 237   2 033200.00
 26410 BEAL, A.M.       470581134 770215 F S B 415   2 034900.00
 37148 THOMAS, W.W.     372587148 750815 M M D 557   2 057900.00
 87613 WATSON, H.T.     885747613 830103 F S B 639   2 027500.00
                        ..... END REPORT .....
```

(c) Result of the N option.

Figure 4.9 Example of the Binary Find count.

There are several options inherent in the binary find methodology. One noteworthy feature is the ability to generate an itemized report. With an N option to the Binary Find function, a result can be created that shows the number of times a line with a given value exists in the report. Figure 4.9 serves as an illustrative example. The count is to be made on the field titled DPT, and the count of lines with a unique DPT value is to be placed in a field titled JOB CLS. In the function mask, the letter "k" denotes the field containing items to count, and the equals sign (=) specifies the field in which to place the count.

As with other inquiry and update functions, the Binary Find function can be applied to a single report or an entire form type.

The Match Function

The *Match function* matches the contents of specified fields from two different reports, similar to a merge or collate operation in traditional data processing. This function creates a "result" report allowing a variety of options. The most commonly used form of the Match function is to compare fields between reports, and then move data values from the sending to the receiving report.

The Match function is invoked by displaying the receiving report, then entering the keyword MA in the control line, and then transmitting it to the computer. The MAPPER system responds with the following script to enter the sending report:

```
MATCH AND EXTRACT
        MODE  ■  ,
    PASSWORD    ,
      FORMAT    ,
         RID          ,
        TYPE    ,
```

Thus, the sending RID can be in a different mode from the receiving RID. The user supplies the requested information and transmits the entire screen to the computer. The MAPPER system responds with a function mask, as with other inquiry and update functions.

Figure 4.10 gives an example of an order list in which the customer number is repeated, meaning that a single customer has placed more than one order. The customer name and state must be retrieved from an associated customer list with unique entries. The objective of the Match function is to match the customer number in the order list with customer number in the customer list, and move the customer name and state to the order list.

The receiving report (ORDER LIST) and sending report (CUSTOMER LIST) are given in Figure 4.10(a) and 4.10(b), respectively. The function mask is given in Figure 4.10(c) and it shows the field to be matched (denoted by the digit 1) and the fields to be moved (denoted by the letters A and B). The result is shown in Figure 4.10(d), and it effectively demonstrates the *join operation* in relational database management.

```
.DATE 23 MAR 83  10:19:34  RID    48    23 MAR 83
.                 ORDER LIST
*ORD. DATE .CUS. CUSTOMER NAME .ST.AMOUNT.
*NUM.      .NUM.                .  .      .
*===.======.===.================.==.======.
 687 830115 528                       12630
 688 830122 320                      471146
 689 830209 733                       86546
 690 830228 633                      101094
 691 830315 320                      233405
 692 830320 528                       61500
 693 830322 320                        2160
                  ..... END REPORT .....
```

(a) Receiving report.

```
.DATE 23 MAR 83  10:27:55  RID    49    23 MAR 83
.        CUSTOMER LIST
*CUS. CUSTOMER NAME .ST.
*NUM.               .  .
*===.================.==.
 320 ACE ALUMINUM    NY
 528 GOOD STEEL      PA
 633 ALPHA MFG       CA
 733 FASTENERS INC   NC
                  ..... END REPORT .....
```

(b) Sending report.

```
.        CUSTOMER LIST
*CUS. CUSTOMER NAME .ST.
*NUM.               .  .
*===.================.==.
 *** **************** **
 1    a               b
.                 ORDER LIST
*ORD. DATE .CUS. CUSTOMER NAME .ST.AMOUNT.
*NUM.      .NUM.                .  .      .
*===.======.===.================.==.======.
 *** ****** *** **************** ** ******
                1    a               b
```

(c) Match function mask.

```
line  1      fmt    rl        shft      hld chrs      hld ln
.
.       7 LINES MATCHED OUT OF     7 LINES

.DATE 23 MAR 83  10:19:34  RID    48    23 MAR 83  JORG
.                 ORDER LIST
*ORD. DATE .CUS. CUSTOMER NAME .ST.AMOUNT.
*NUM.      .NUM.                .  .      .
*===.======.===.================.==.======.
 687 830115 528 GOOD STEEL      PA  12630
 688 830122 320 ACE ALUMINUM    NY 471146
 689 830209 733 FASTENERS INC   NC  86546
 690 830228 633 ALPHA MFG       CA 101094
 691 830315 320 ACE ALUMINUM    NY 233405
 692 830320 528 GOOD STEEL      PA  61500
 693 830322 320 ACE ALUMINUM    NY   2160
                  ..... END REPORT .....
```

(d) Result.

Figure 4.10 Example of the Match function with the move option.

With the Match function, there can be up to five match fields (specified by the digits 1 through 5) and up to 13 fields moved (specified by the letters A through M). Some of the options available with the Match function are given as follows:

- Delete matched data in the receiving report.
- Do not fill moved fields on no match cases.
- Make the sending report the report that is initially on display.
- Display only matched lines.
- Display only no-match lines.
- Matched fields are in sorted order.
- Display matched lines in sending report order.

The Match function gives the capability of performing a comprehensive data processing function, usually requiring a complete program, with a single MAPPER command.

Overview of Other Manual Functions

As listed in Table 4.1, there are at least 39 manual functions that could be introduced. Some are heavily used and others are infrequently invoked. Moreover, several functions relate to the operational environment of system software.

Five additional functions, contained in Table 4.1, have a definite data processing emphasis:

- Change.
- Match update.
- Search list.
- Search list and update.
- Search update.

A short description of these functions is given in the following paragraph.

The *Change function* matches and changes strings of characters in a report. The *Match Update function* permits the receiving report of a match operation to be physically updated. Normally, a result report is created from the Match function. The *Search List function* allows a search operation to be performed using parameters from another report. The *Search List Update function* permits a report to be physically updated as a result of the search operation using the list option, and the *Search Update function* provides a similar result without the list option.

It is important to recognize that the MAPPER system has evolved as a result of actual user involvement in the design process. Without end-user input, software development for end-user computing can easily become an academic endeavor.

Summary

Visual programming normally refers to two conditions: the ability to conveniently look at a complete data structure, and a means of specifying options and parameters in relation to the associated data structure. In the MAPPER system, visual programming is provided by facilities for easily displaying a report, and by using a function mask for entering function parameters. Most inquiry and update functions utilize a function mask that is entered visually or lexically in the fast-access mode.

In a lengthy or complex report, it is cumbersome to visually search for the first data line that meets a given condition. Finding subsequent data lines can be equally tedious. The *Find function* searches for the first occurrence of specified data in a report or form type. RIDs can be chained so that after one report has been searched, a succeeding one is referenced. The Find function is display-oriented, because the operation finds the first occurrence of a required data line and places it as the first data line on the screen. This is effectively a scrolling operation, and the report can be ROLLed up or down from that point.

The *Search function* scans an entire report or form type for "all" lines that satisfy a specified condition and produces a "result" report. The search operation can be applied to a single or several RIDs chained together. This function incorporates several options, such as range searching and inverse searching. The result report of a search operation may be used as input to other MAPPER functions.

Since most MAPPER functions perform column-dependent operations, a means is needed to perform a search operation on a column-independent basis. The *Locate function* performs a column-independent scan of a report, similar in concept to the find function. This function performs a column-independent search of a report using a specified character string as a search argument. The first data line meeting the specified conditions is ROLLed to the first data line position on the screen. The Locate function does not generate a new report as a result.

The *Sort function* can be used to reorder lines in a report or in a result on display. The sort operation can be based on single or multiple fields, and in ascending or descending order. Moreover, fields may be character-oriented or numeric. The Sort function always produces a result report.

The *Binary Find function* applies "binary search" logic to the Find function, and is particularly efficient for large-sized RIDs. A sorted search key is sampled at interval midpoints to reduce search time. The Binary Find function produces the same result as the conventional Find function; the primary difference is that the search key *must* be sorted. There are several options to this command. One noteworthy feature is the ability to generate an itemized report counting the number of occurrences of a specified condition or data value.

The *Match function* matches the contents of specified fields from two different reports in the same manner that merge and collate operations work in conventional data processing. A result report, based on a "receiving report," is created, and a common option is to move data values from a sending to the receiving report for matched data lines. The Match function gives the capability of performing a comprehensive data processing function, usually requiring a complete program, with a single MAPPER command.

Five Additional manual functions have a data processing orientation: Change, Match Update, Search List, Search List Update, and Search Update. Through the addition of functions such as these, the MAPPER system has evolved as a result of actual user involvement in the design process.

CHAPTER FIVE

MAPPER Calculations

A report processing system is incomplete without the capability of performing arithmetic operations on single values and tabular data. The MAPPER system includes an Arithmetic function for routine calculations and a Totalize function for horizontal and vertical arithmetic, as well as for movement, subtotaling, summation, cumulation, entry counting, sequencing, and averaging. As with most MAPPER functions, there are several options to the Arithmetic and Totalize commands. The most commonly used operations are presented.

Calculator Facility

The Arithmetic function provides a calculator facility for performing mathematical computations. The following mathematical operations are accepted by the MAPPER system:

Operation	Symbol	Form
Addition	+	a+b
Subtraction	−	a−b
Multiplication	*	a*b
Division	/	a/b
Exponentiation	**	a**b
Negation	−	−a

Expressions take the same form as in commonly-used programming languages, such as BASIC and FORTRAN. The following hierarchy of operations is defined:

Operation	Symbol	Hierarchy
Unary minus	–	High
Exponentiation	**	
Multiplication, Division	*,/	
Addition, Subtraction	+,–	Low

As a result of this operation hierarchy, the expression 2+3*4 has a value of 14, since multiplication is performed before addition. Parentheses may be used for grouping and to specify an order of execution.

The *Arithmetic function* is invoked by entering the keyword A in the control line and transmitting it to the computer. The MAPPER system responds with the screen given in Figure 5.1. An expression is simply entered after the Start-of-Entry (SOF) character (▶), and transmitted to the computer. The MAPPER system performs the specified calculations and stores the result in a variable for use in subsequent expressions. Variable names are assigned successively as single letters, starting with A and progressing through Z. A user may choose meaningful names composed of up to six alphabetic characters.

Figure 5.2, screens 1 through 3, depicts successive calculator operations. In the arithmetic mode, new expressions are always entered at the top of the screen.

2+2

```
                    *** MAPPER 1100 ***
                    ARITHMETIC CALCULATOR

             ENTER FORTRAN TYPE EQUATION FOLLOWING THE
             CURSOR AND TRANSMIT FOR COMPUTATION AND ANSWER
```

Figure 5.1 Initial screen for the Arithmetic function and a simple expression.

```
2+2
 A  =              4
```

```
          *** MAPPER 1100 ***
          ARITHMETIC CALCULATOR

     ENTER FORTRAN TYPE EQUATION FOLLOWING THE
     CURSOR AND TRANSMIT FOR COMPUTATION AND ANSWER
```

(a) Screen 1.

```
2+3*A
 B  =             14
2+2
 A  =              4
```

```
          *** MAPPER 1100 ***
          ARITHMETIC CALCULATOR

     ENTER FORTRAN TYPE EQUATION FOLLOWING THE
     CURSOR AND TRANSMIT FOR COMPUTATION AND ANSWER
```

(b) Screen 2.

```
B/2+A
 C  =             11
2+3*A
 B  =             14
2+2
 A  =              4
```

```
          *** MAPPER 1100 ***
          ARITHMETIC CALCULATOR

     ENTER FORTRAN TYPE EQUATION FOLLOWING THE
     CURSOR AND TRANSMIT FOR COMPUTATION AND ANSWER
```

(c) Screen 3.

Figure 5.2 Successive screens for the Arithmetic function. (Screens should be read 1 through 3.)

Arithmetic expressions can be predefined and placed in a Type A RID for execution by the MAPPER system. The root of a quadratic equation is defined as follows:

```
A=1
B=5
C=6
ROOT=(-B+SQRT(B**2-4*A*C) )/2*A
```

```
.DATE 23 MAR 83  11:44:41  RID      53    23 MAR 83
.EXECUTION OF PREDEFINED EXPRESSIONS
*=====================================================

 A=1;
 B=5;
 C=6;
 ROOT=(-B+SQRT(B**2-4*A*C))/2*A;



              ..... END REPORT .....
```

(a) Free form RID for the Arithmetic function.

```
                       Arithmetic function active
 A=1;
 B=5;
 C=6;
 ROOT=(-B+SQRT(B**2-4*A*C))/2*A;

 A=1;
 B=5;
 C=6;
 ROOT=(-B+SQRT(B**2-4*A*C))/2*A;
 ROOT =              -2
```

(b) Result.

Figure 5.3 Execution of predefined expressions with the
            Arithmetic function.

This set of calculations is placed in a RID, as shown in Figure 5.3(a), and executed by entering the fast-access command:

A rt

in the control line and transmitting it to the computer. In this case, "rt" is a RID/type designation. In the above example, the MAPPER system responds with the screen given in Figure 5.3(b). In the computer version of this problem, a tab character precedes each line, and each line ends with a semicolon.

The Arithmetic function in MAPPER includes several mathematical and trigonometric functions, such as the square root (SQRT), to facilitate everyday calculations.

Totalize Function Overview

The Totalize function gives the MAPPER user the ability to perform calculations on tabular data. More specifically, arithmetic and move operations can be executed on data fields within reports or results on a horizontal basis (e.g. column operations), and summary calculations, such as averaging and subtotaling, can be performed on a vertical basis. The Totalize function can be applied to any displayed report; in fact, the Totalize function can be applied to the result of a previous Totalize function.

The Totalize function is invoked by displaying the report to be processed and entering the keyword TOT in the control line and transmitting it to the computer. The MAPPER system responds with a function mask that permits the parameter symbols to be entered. For horizontal operations, the following symbols can be used:

Symbol	Horizontal Operation
+	Addition
-	Subtraction
*	Multiplication
/	Division
=	Result
M	Move

For vertical operations, the symbols assume a slightly different meaning:

Symbol	Vertical Operation
+	Vertical Summation and Entry Counting
S	Subtotaling
C	Cumulation and Sequencing
A	Averaging
=	Filling Fields

Two standard reports are used for examples of the various operations. The *money report*, listed in Figure 5.4, is used for calculations involving data movement, additive operations, vertical summation, cumulation, and averaging. The *order report*, listed in Figure 5.5, is used for calculations involving multiplicative operations and subtotaling.

```
.DATE 23 MAR 83  11:13:21  RID     51    23 MAR 83
.                       MONEY REPORT
*EMPLY.    EMPLOYEE    . SALES  . BONUS .EXPENSES.  TOTAL  .
* NUM .     NAME       .        .       .        .        .
*=====.================.=========.========.========.=========.
 12097 JAMES, R.C.      71500.00  7150.00    715.00
 26410 BEAL, A.M.       41250.50  4125.05    412.50
 37148 THOMAS, W.W.      8100.75   810.07     81.00
 42635 BORDER, S.K.   121750.00 24350.00  12175.00
                     ..... END REPORT .....
```

Figure 5.4 Money Report to be used with several Totalize functions.

```
.DATE 23 MAR 83  11:30:36  RID      52    23 MAR 83
.         ORDER REPORT
*ORDER.UNIT.UNIT.UNIT.QUAN.AMOUNT.
*NUMBR.NUMB.NAME. PR .    .      .
*=====.====.====.====.=====.======.
    111     5 AAAA   10     5
    111     6 BBBB   20     2
    222     7 CCCC   15     3
    222     8 DDDD   25     3
    222     9 EEEE   50     1
    333     6 BBBB   20    10
    333     8 DDDD   25     2
                    ..... END REPORT .....
```

Figure 5.5 Order Report.

Horizontal Movement

As a non-arithmetic case of the Totalize function, data can be moved from one column to another with the move option. After the function mask is received on the screen, the letter M is placed in the column to be moved, and an equal sign (=) is placed in the receiving field. This case is demonstrated on the Money Report in Figure 5.6, wherein the SALES field is moved to the TOTAL field.

```
.                      MONEY REPORT
*EMPLY.   EMPLOYEE   . SALES  . BONUS .EXPENSES.  TOTAL  .
* NUM .     NAME     .        .       .        .         .
*=====.============== .=========.========.=========.=========.
***** ************** ********* ******** ******** *********
                     m                            =
```

(a) Function mask for horizontal movement.

```
.DATE 23 MAR 83  11:13:21  RID      51    23 MAR 83
.                      MONEY REPORT
*EMPLY.   EMPLOYEE   . SALES  . BONUS .EXPENSES.  TOTAL  .
* NUM .     NAME     .        .       .        .         .
*=====.============== .=========.========.=========.=========.
 12097 JAMES, R.C.      71500.00  7150.00    715.00  71500.00
 26410 BEAL, A.M.       41250.50  4125.05    412.50  41250.50
 37148 THOMAS, W.W.      8100.75   810.07     81.00   8100.75
 42635 BORDER, S.K.    121750.00 24350.00  12175.00 121750.00
                    ..... END REPORT .....
```

(b) Result.

Figure 5.6 Example of horizontal movement.

Horizontal Arithmetic

The horizontal arithmetic option provides the capability of performing calculations on a column-wise basis and then replacing the contents of another column with the result. The following procedure applies after the function mask is presented:

- A function symbol, such as + or –, should be entered into the first character position of fields that should participate in the arithmetic operations.

- An equal sign (=) should be entered in the first character position of the field into which the result should be placed.

After the entire screen containing the function mask is transmitted to the computer, the MAPPER system responds with the displayed report, including the results of the specified arithmetic operations.

Figure 5.7 contains an example of horizontal addition and subtraction applied to the *Money Report*, in which the following sequence of calculations is performed:

SALES+BONUS–EXPENSES=TOTAL

```
.                      MONEY REPORT
*EMPLY.     EMPLOYEE     .  SALES  .  BONUS .EXPENSES.   TOTAL   .
* NUM .       NAME       .         .        .         .          .
*=====. ===============. =========. ========.=========. =========.
***** ************** ******** ******** ******** ********
                         +         +         -         =
```

(a) Function mask for horizontal addition and subtraction.

```
.DATE 23 MAR 83  11:13:21  RID      51    23 MAR 83
.                      MONEY REPORT
*EMPLY.     EMPLOYEE     .  SALES  .  BONUS .EXPENSES.   TOTAL   .
* NUM .       NAME       .         .        .         .          .
*=====. ===============. =========. ========.=========. =========.
 12097 JAMES, R.C.        71500.00  7150.00   715.00 77935.000
 26410 BEAL, A.M.         41250.50  4125.05   412.50 44963.050
 37148 THOMAS, W.W.        8100.75   810.07    81.00 8829.8200
 42635 BORDER, S.K.      121750.00 24350.00 12175.00 133925.00
                   ..... END REPORT .....
```

(b) Result.

Figure 5.7 Example of horizontal arithmetic involving addition and subtraction applied to the Money Report.

```
.              ORDER REPORT
*ORDER.UNIT.UNIT.UNIT.QUAN.AMOUNT.
*NUMBR.NUMB.NAME. PR .    .      .
*=====.====.====.====.====.======.
 ***** **** **** **** **** ******
                  +     *    =
```

(a) Function mask for horizontal multiplication.

```
.DATE 23 MAR 83  11:30:36  RID     52    23 MAR 83
.              ORDER REPORT
*ORDER.UNIT.UNIT.UNIT.QUAN.AMOUNT.
*NUMBR.NUMB.NAME. PR .    .      .
*=====.====.====.====.====.======.
  111    5 AAAA  10    5     50
  111    6 BBBB  20    2     40
  222    7 CCCC  15    3     45
  222    8 DDDD  25    3     75
  222    9 EEEE  50    1     50
  333    6 BBBB  20   10    200
  333    8 DDDD  25    2     50
                 ..... END REPORT .....
```

(b) Result.

Figure 5.8 Example of horizontal arithmetic involving multiplication applied to the Order Report.

The function mask in Figure 5.7(a) contains a plus sign under SALES and BONUS, and a minus sign under EXPENSES, and should be interpreted as follows: Take SALES, add BONUS, and subtract EXPENSES. The result is placed in TOTAL, because that is where the equal sign is placed. As many as 16 operators can be placed on a single parameter line.

Figure 5.8 contains an example of horizontal multiplication applied to the *Order Report,* in which the following sequence of calculations is performed:

UNIT PRICE*QUAN=AMT

The function mask in Figure 5.8(a) contains a plus sign under UNIT PRICE, and an asterisk for multiplication under QUAN, and should be interpreted as follows: Take UNIT PRICE and multiply it by QUAN. The result is placed in AMT, because that is where the equal sign is placed.

Only one multiplication, division, or move operation may be placed on a single parameter line.

Arithmetic operations involving a numeric constant are indicated by placing the operator and constant under the field participating in the operation. Assume in the Order Report that it were necessary to multiply each UNIT PRICE by the number 2 and place the result temporarily in the AMT column, as follows:

```
.                ORDER REPORT
*ORDER.UNIT.UNIT.UNIT.QUAN.AMOUNT.
*NUMBR.NUMB.NAME. PR .    .       .
*=====.====.====.====.====.======.
 ***** **** **** **** **** ******
                 *2           =
```

(a) Function mask for horizontal multiplication by a constant.

```
.DATE 23 MAR 83  11:30:36  RID     52    23 MAR 83
.                ORDER REPORT
*ORDER.UNIT.UNIT.UNIT.QUAN.AMOUNT.
*NUMBR.NUMB.NAME. PR .    .       .
*=====.====.====.====.====.======.
  111   5 AAAA   10    5     20
  111   6 BBBB   20    2     40
  222   7 CCCC   15    3     30
  222   8 DDDD   25    3     50
  222   9 EEEE   50    1    100
  333   6 BBBB   20   10     40
  333   8 DDDD   25    2     50
               ..... END REPORT .....
```

(b) Result.

Figure 5.9 Example of horizontal multiplication by a constant applied to the Order Report.

UNIT PRICE*2=AMT

The function mask in Figure 5.9(a) contains an asterisk for multiplication, and the constant 2 under UNIT PRICE, and should be interpreted as follows: Multiply UNIT PRICE by two. The result is placed in AMT, because that is where the equal sign is placed. In this case, AMT is used as a temporary column; the contents of AMT could be moved back to UNIT PRICE with horizontal movement.

Vertical Summation

Vertical Summation is the process of totaling columns of data in a report. The result is listed at the bottom of the report. Summation can be combined with horizontal arithmetic operations in the same parameter specification.

To invoke Vertical Summation, the report is displayed, and the keyword TOT is entered in the control line and transmitted to the computer, as covered above. When the function mask is displayed, plus signs are entered in columns to be summed, as shown for the Money Report in Figure 5.10. Columns labeled SALES, BONUS, and EXPENSES are added because plus signs are placed below them.

```
.                       MONEY REPORT
*EMPLY.    EMPLOYEE    .  SALES  .  BONUS .EXPENSES.  TOTAL  .
* NUM .      NAME      .         .        .        .         .
*=====.===============.=========.========.========.=========.
***** *************** ********* ******** ******** *********
                          +        +        +
```

(a) Function mask for vertical summation.

```
.DATE 23 MAR 83  11:13:21  RID     51    23 MAR 83
.                       MONEY REPORT
*EMPLY.    EMPLOYEE    .  SALES  .  BONUS .EXPENSES.  TOTAL  .
* NUM .      NAME      .         .        .        .         .
*=====.===============.=========.========.========.=========.
 12097 JAMES, R.C.        71500.00  7150.00    715.00
 26410 BEAL, A.M.         41250.50  4125.05    412.50
 37148 THOMAS, W.W.        8100.75   810.07     81.00
 42635 BORDER, S.K.     121750.00 24350.00  12175.00
.
.GRAND-TOTAL   -
.    SALES               = 242601.25000
.    BONUS             = 36435.12000
. EXPENSES            = 13383.50000
                         ..... END REPORT .....
```

(b) Result.

Figure 5.10 Example of vertical summation applied to the
            Money Report.

```
.                       MONEY REPORT
*EMPLY.    EMPLOYEE    .  SALES  .  BONUS .EXPENSES.  TOTAL  .
* NUM .      NAME      .         .        .        .         .
*=====.===============.=========.========.========.=========.
***** *************** ********* ******** ******** *********
                          +        +        -        =
                                                     +
```

(a) Function mask for the Totalize function that specifies both horizontal
arithmetic and vertical summation.

```
.DATE 23 MAR 83  11:13:21  RID     51    23 MAR 83
.                       MONEY REPORT
*EMPLY.    EMPLOYEE    .  SALES  .  BONUS .EXPENSES.  TOTAL  .
* NUM .      NAME      .         .        .        .         .
*=====.===============.=========.========.========.=========.
 12097 JAMES, R.C.        71500.00  7150.00    715.00 77935.000
 26410 BEAL, A.M.         41250.50  4125.05    412.50 44963.050
 37148 THOMAS, W.W.        8100.75   810.07     81.00 8829.8200
 42635 BORDER, S.K.     121750.00 24350.00  12175.00 133925.00
.
.GRAND-TOTAL   -
.    TOTAL             = 265652.87000
                         ..... END REPORT .....
```

(b) Result.

Figure 5.11 Example of horizontal arithmetic and vertical summation
            applied to the Money Report.

Vertical summation and horizontal arithmetic can be combined, as demonstrated in Figure 5.11. In this case, the sequence of calculations, previously described as:

SALES+BONUS-EXPENSES=TOTAL

is performed on a column-by-column basis. Then, the column labeled TOTAL is summed, because a plus sign is placed below the equal sign in the function mask in Figure 5.11(a).

Subtotaling

A vertical summation of data fields for groups of related data is referred to as *Subtotaling.* In order to perform a subtotal operation, two items of information are necessary: a key field with a control break and a set of fields to be subtotaled. As before, subtotaling is invoked with the keyword TOT for a displayed report.

Subtotaling is specified in the function mask by placing the letter S in the key field and a plus sign under fields to be subtotaled. The basic idea is that each time the key field changes, i.e. a control break occurs, a subtotal is produced.

Figure 5.12 demonstrates the application of subtotaling to the Order Report. A complete version of the input is given in Figure 5.12(a). The key field is ORD NUM, and the field to be subtotaled is AMT. Figure

```
.DATE 23 MAR 83  11:30:36  RID      52     23 MAR 83
.              ORDER REPORT
*ORDER.UNIT.UNIT.UNIT.QUAN.AMOUNT.
*NUMBR.NUMB.NAME. PR .    .       .
*=====.====.====.====.====.======.
   111     5 AAAA   10    5     50
   111     6 BBBB   20    2     40
   222     7 CCCC   15    3     45
   222     8 DDDD   25    3     75
   222     9 EEEE   50    1     50
   333     6 BBBB   20   10    200
   333     8 DDDD   25    2     50
                   ..... END REPORT .....
```

(a) Completed version of the Order Report.

```
.              ORDER REPORT
*ORDER.UNIT.UNIT.UNIT.QUAN.AMOUNT.
*NUMBR.NUMB.NAME. PR .    .       .
*=====.====.====.====.====.======.
 ***** **** **** **** **** ******
  s                          +
```

(b) Function mask.

```
.DATE              13:52:15  RID      52    23 MAR 83
.              ORDER REPORT
*ORDER.UNIT.UNIT.UNIT.QUAN.AMOUNT.
*NUMBR.NUMB.NAME. PR .      .        .
*=====.====.====.====.=====.======.
   111      5 AAAA   10      5       50
   111      6 BBBB   20      2       40
.SUBTOTAL   -    ORDER NUMBR =     111
. AMOUNT         =        90
   222      7 CCCC   15      3       45
   222      8 DDDD   25      3       75
   222      9 EEEE   50      1       50
.SUBTOTAL   -    ORDER NUMBR =     222
. AMOUNT         =       170
   333      6 BBBB   20     10      200
   333      8 DDDD   25      2       50
.SUBTOTAL   -    ORDER NUMBR =     333
. AMOUNT         =       250
.
.GRAND-TOTAL   -
. AMOUNT         =       510
           ..... END REPORT .....
```

(c) Result.

Figure 5.12 Example of subtotaling applied to the Order Report.

5.12(b) gives the function wherein the letter S is placed in the ORD NUM
column and a plus sign is placed in the AMT column. The result is given
as Figure 5.12(c).

Averaging

The *averaging* option to the Totalize function computes the average of
a column of data values, and prints the result at the end of the report.
The specifications for averaging are entered when the function mask for
the TOT command is displayed.

To specify averaging in the function mask, the letter A is placed in the
first column of fields to be averaged. During the computation, the MAP-
PER system performs a vertical summation of the data values in a column
and divides that result by the number of entries.

Figure 5.13 demonstrates the application of averaging to the Money
Report. A completed version of the report is given in Figure 5.13(a). The
columns to be averaged are SALES, BONUS, EXPENSES, and TOTAL.
Figure 5.13(b) gives the function mask wherein the letter A is placed in
columns to be averaged. The result is given in 5.13(c). Clearly, the result

is displayed in text form below a display of the report. By including an "s" option in line 0 of the function mask, as in Figure 5.13(d), the averages are displayed below their respective columns, as in Figure 5.13(e).

```
.DATE 23 MAR 83  11:13:21  RID     51    23 MAR 83
                        MONEY REPORT
*EMPLY.    EMPLOYEE    . SALES  . BONUS .EXPENSES.  TOTAL  .
* NUM .     NAME       .        .       .        .         .
*=====.================.=========.========.========.=========.
 12097 JAMES, R.C.      71500.00  7150.00    715.00 77935.000
 26410 BEAL, A.M.       41250.50  4125.05    412.50 44963.050
 37148 THOMAS, W.W.      8100.75   810.07     81.00 8829.8200
 42635 BORDER, S.K.    121750.00 24350.00  12175.00 133925.00
                       ..... END REPORT .....
```

(a) Completed version of the Money Report.

```
.                      MONEY REPORT
*EMPLY.    EMPLOYEE    . SALES  . BONUS .EXPENSES.  TOTAL  .
* NUM .     NAME       .        .       .        .         .
*=====.================.=========.========.========.=========.
*****  **************** ********* ******** ******** *********
                           a         a        a        a
```

(b) Function mask.

```
.DATE            13:56:46  RID     51    23 MAR 83
                        MONEY REPORT
*EMPLY.    EMPLOYEE    . SALES  . BONUS .EXPENSES.  TOTAL  .
* NUM .     NAME       .        .       .        .         .
*=====.================.=========.========.========.=========.
 12097 JAMES, R.C.      71500.00  7150.00    715.00 77935.000
 26410 BEAL, A.M.       41250.50  4125.05    412.50 44963.050
 37148 THOMAS, W.W.      8100.75   810.07     81.00 8829.8200
 42635 BORDER, S.K.    121750.00 24350.00  12175.00 133925.00
.
.GRAND-TOTAL   -
.    SALES          - AVERAGE = 60650.312500
.    BONUS          - AVERAGE = 9108.780000.
.    EXPENSES       - AVERAGE = 3345.875000
.    TOTAL          - AVERAGE = 66413.217500
                    ..... END REPORT .....
```

(c) Result displayed below the report.

```
s
.                      MONEY REPORT
*EMPLY.    EMPLOYEE    . SALES  . BONUS .EXPENSES.  TOTAL  .
* NUM .     NAME       .        .       .        .         .
*=====.================.=========.========.========.=========.
*****  **************** ********* ******** ******** *********
                           a         a        a        a
```

(d) Function mask with the "s" option for column placement.

```
.DATE              13:56:46  RID    51    23 MAR 83
.                     MONEY REPORT
*EMPLY.    EMPLOYEE  . SALES  .  BONUS .EXPENSES.  TOTAL  .
* NUM .     NAME     .        .        .         .        .
*=====. ==============. =========.=========.=========.==========.
 12097 JAMES, R.C.    71500.00  7150.00   715.00 77935.000
 26410 BEAL, A.M.     41250.50  4125.05   412.50 44963.050
 37148 THOMAS, W.W.    8100.75   810.07    81.00 8829.8200
 42635 BORDER, S.K.  121750.00 24350.00 12175.00 133925.00
.
.GRAND-TOTAL   -
*
                     60650.313 9108.780 3345.875 66413.218
                 ..... END REPORT .....
```

(e) Results displayed below their respective columns.

Figure 5.13 Example of averaging applied to the Money Report.

Overview of Other Totalize Function Operations

As with other MAPPER functions, there are a variety of alternatives to the Totalize function. Five additional options are worth noting:

- Cumulation.
- Entry counting.
- Sequencing.
- Rounding.
- Filling fields.

A short description of these options is given in the following paragraph. The *cumulative option* repetitively adds a data value to a running total and saves the total in a column position. The *entry counting option* counts the number of entries in a column. This option is often necessary because data fields are not always filled. The *sequencing option* allows the user to number data lines in a column. The increment for sequencing may be specified. The *rounding option* provides the capability of scaling and rounding the data values participating in a Totalize function. The *filling fields option* permits fields to be filled with a specified value.

Facilities for performing calculations are adequate to the needs of a report processing system. Extensive mathematical capability is not available.

Summary

The Arithmetic function in MAPPER provides a calculator facility for performing mathematical computations. MAPPER accepts the following mathematical operations:

Operation	Symbol	Form
Addition	+	a+b
Subtraction	–	a–b
Multiplication	*	a*b
Division	/	a/b
Exponentiation	**	a**b
Negation	–	–a

Expressions take the same form as in languages like BASIC and FORTRAN. The Arithmetic function accepts expressions interactively or as predefined Type A RIDs.

The Totalize function provides the capability of performing "spreadsheet like" calculations on tabular data. Operations can be performed on reports or results. Calculations can be executed horizontally on a column-by-column basis or vertically for summary results, such as totaling, subtotaling, and averaging. The following operation symbols are defined for horizontal operations:

Operator Symbol	Horizontal Operation
+	Addition
–	Subtraction
*	Multiplication
/	Division
=	Result placement
M	Column movement

For vertical operations, the symbols assume a slightly different meaning:

Operator Symbol	Vertical Operation
+	Vertical summation or entry counting
S	Subtotaling
C	Cumulation and Sequencing
A	Averaging
=	Field Filling

The operator symbols on the previous page are used in field positions in the function mask for the Totalize function.

Horizontal movement is a non-arithmetic use of the Totalize function. With this function, the contents of data fields in one column position can be moved to another column position.

The horizontal arithmetic option to the Totalize function provides the capability of performing calculations on a column-by-column basis, and then replacing the contents of another column with the result. As covered above, a function mask is used for this purpose. In a single mask, as many as 16 operators can be placed on a single line of the mask, denoting 16 different arithmetic operations. The only exceptions are the multiplication and division symbols, which are limited to one per line. Horizontal arithmetic operations may also incorporate constant values.

Vertical summation is the process of totaling columns of data in a report. The result is listed at the bottom of the report. Summation can be combined with horizontal arithmetic operations in the same parameter specification in the Totalize function mask to produce a vertical summation of the result column.

A vertical summation of data fields for groups of related data is referred to as *Subtotaling.* In order to perform a subtotal operation, two items of information are necessary: a key field with a control break, and a set of fields to be subtotaled.

The Averaging option to the Totalize function computes the average of a column of data values, and prints the result at the end of the report or below the respective column, depending upon how the operation is specified in the function mask. During the computation, the MAPPER system performs a vertical summation of the data values in a column and divides that result by the number of entries.

Five additional alternatives to the Totalize function are important for arithmetic in a report processing environment:

- Cumulation.
- Entry counting.
- Sequencing.
- Rounding.
- Filling fields.

While extensive mathematical capability is not a part of MAPPER, the arithmetic facilities are more than sufficient for its application domain.

CHAPTER SIX

MAPPER Run Facility

Many data processing operations involve not only a single MAPPER command, such as Search or Totalize, but a series of MAPPER commands entered successively. During actual use, it then becomes tedious to enter the procedure repetitively, and the entire process is highly susceptible to errors of various kinds. In some cases, the functions are too complex to be entered manually, and in other cases, the occasional user does not have enough day-to-day experience with MAPPER to enter commands successfully. In situations such as this, it is convenient to prepare a meaningful list of MAPPER commands, giving a step-by-step procedure for solving a data processing or reporting requirement, and store that list in the MAPPER system under a meaningful name. From then on, the end-user can execute the series of commands by using the assigned name. A procedure of this type is called a *run* in MAPPER. It is commonplace in computer installations using the MAPPER system for an experienced MAPPER user to prepare runs for execution by inexperienced persons and occasional users.

The Run Concept

A *run* is a set of run control statements that give the step-by-step procedure to perform a specific set of data processing operations or a report generation. A run control statement is essentially a MAPPER command along with its parameters specified in a free form line, such as the following Add Report statement:

@ADR,20,250 . COMMENT – ADD REPORT STATEMENT

Each line begins with the "at" sign (@) and ends with a period. Comments may follow the period, which must be preceded by a space character.

All manual commands have counterparts as run control statements. In addition the run facility in MAPPER contains statements that deal with the automatic mode of operation, such as the capability for performing conditional logic and input/output. The run control statements composing a run are stored as free form lines in a RID; the RID is assigned a run name that is registered with the MAPPER coordinator, so that security and various authorization conventions can be maintained. A run is executed by entering its name in the control line and transmitting it to the computer.

A run is executed by the MAPPER run control facility by successively selecting statements, interpreting them, and then executing them. The major difference between the manual and automatic modes is evident. A run control statement must be self contained, since user interaction is not permitted at the command level. Clearly, data can be entered into and displayed from an executing run.

Most MAPPER run control statements appear to be difficult to read because of the extensive use of positional parameters. Appearance is misleading, however, since a statement format is a direct mapping of its manual counterpart, and most forms are easily remembered. Each run control line begins with the "at" sign (@), but may contain any number of MAPPER commands and periods before the terminal period character (.). The MAPPER system works most efficiently with run control lines that are 80 characters or less and have multiple commands per line. Run control lines may contain up to 132 characters, but their use is not recommended.

Run Control Line

Run control statements have a fixed format that is consistently applied, and specific terminology applies to the run control line and to the statement format. Figure 6.1 gives the terminology for the parts of a run

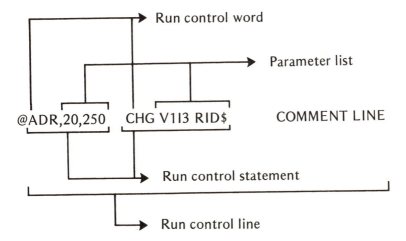

Figure 6.1 Terminology for parts of a run control line.

control line. The control word is the keyword used to denote a statement. The control words are grouped by the functions they perform into the following categories:

- Report update functions.
- Line update functions.
- Computational functions.
- Terminal manipulation functions.
- Run termination functions.
- Inquiry functions.
- Miscellaneous.

The control words for a representative set of run control statements is listed in Table 6.1. The following statements are covered here:

Control Word	Function
ADR	Add report
DLR	Delete report
DSP	Display report

Control Word	Function
DUP	Duplicate report
REP	Replace report
RNM	Rename report
TOT	Arithmetic operations
MCH	Match and move data from sending to receiving report
SOR	Sort report
SRH	Search report

The above statements were selected because they have a well-defined manual counterpart and allow the user to "think manual," more so than some of the other commands. Moreover, the manual counterparts of these commands were presented earlier.

Table 6.1 Representative Set of Run Control Statements

Command	Function
REPORT UPDATE FUNCTIONS	
ADR	Add a report
BRK	Make the run output area a report
DLR	Delete a report
DSP	Display a report at the terminal
DUP	Duplicate a report
REP	Replace a report
RFM	Reformat a report
RNM	Rename a report
LINE-UPDATE FUNCTIONS	
DEL	Delete lines from a report used with the report update functions
LLN	Locate the last line in a report
LNX	Duplicate lines within a report
LN+	Add lines to a report
LN–	Delete line from a report
RDC	Read lines continuously from a report
RDL	Read a line from a report

Table 6.1 continued

Command   *Function*

LINE UPDATE FUNCTIONS (continued)

RLN   Read the next line from a report

WRL   Write a line within a report

COMPUTATIONAL FUNCTIONS

ART   Perform arithmetic (arithmetic calculator)

CHG   Change the contents of a variable

DAT   Perform arithmetics on dates within a report

SUB   Create subtotals within a report

TOT   Perform arithmetic functions in a report

TERMINAL MANIPULATION FUNCTIONS

DLL   Down line load software into a UTS 400

DSP   Display a report on the terminal

OUT   Output information to the terminal

REL   Release the terminal

SEN   Send a message to a terminal

TCS   Transfer data to and from tape cassette

XIT   Sign the user off the terminal

RUN TERMINATION FUNCTIONS

End of report   Logically arriving at the end of the report that
                contains the run will terminate the run

GTO END   Go to end (a label signifying the end of any run)

REL   Releasing the terminal will terminate a run

RTN   Return a report from a remote system and
             terminate the remote run

XIT   Signing the user off the terminal will end the run

INQUIRY FUNCTIONS

CES   Display the communications error summary

FND   Find data within a report

LCH   Locate and change data within a report

LOC   Locate data within a report

Table 6.1 continued

Command	Function
Command	*Function*

INQUIRY FUNCTIONS (continued)

Command	Function
LOG	Log each function executed in a run
MAU	Match, extract, and update a report
MCH	Match and extract data from one report to another
SOR	Sort the specified report
SLU	Search list update a report
SRH	Search a report
SRL	Search list a report
SRU	Search update a report

MISCELLANEOUS FUNCTIONS

Command	Function
AQ	Analyze queue: analyze and alter queued auxiliary reports and messages
AUX	Send a report to a device connected to a terminal auxiliary interface
DEF	Test a variable for character type
GTO	Branch within a report
IF	Logical decision-making
IND	Index the specified form type
INS	Insert data into variables
LOK	Lock the specified report for updating
MOD	Move control to different mode
PRT	Send a report to a printer
RFM	Reformat a report
RRN	Start a run in another MAPPER 1100 system
RUN	Start another RUN function
STR	Start a batch job
ULK	Unlock the specified report from updating
UPD	Update (used after a SRU, MAU, SLU, etc.)
WAT	Wait (stall a run)

Run Control Statement Format

There is no overall statement format for run control statements in MAP-PER; however, the generalized run control statement format given in Figure 6.2 covers the majority of cases and provides an excellent introduction to the concept. The following fields are identified:

- The special at symbol (@) that begins every run control line.

- A control word, identifying the run control statement, e.g. ADR (for Add Report), SRH (for Search), or TOT (for Totalize).

- The mode, type, and RID numbers. In the present version of MAPPER, the type is an octal number. In the future, it is expected that a letter in the range A through I will be permitted.

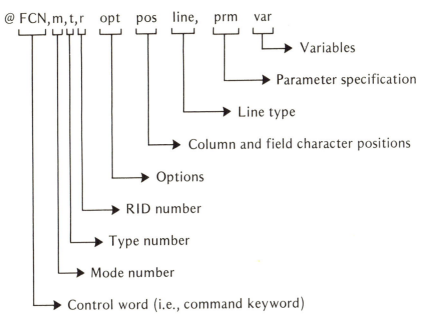

Figure 6.2 Generalized format of a run control statement.

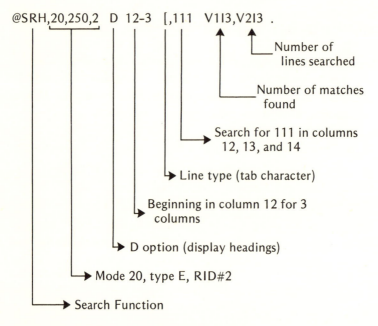

Figure 6.3 Example of the Search function.

- The options field (*opt*) allows the option specifications, normally entered manually, to be given.

- The position field (*pos*) is used to specify the column and field positions in a function mask.

- The line position (*line*) is used to specify the type of line to be considered, e.g. the tab line for the search function.

- The parameters field (*prm*) is used to designate the values normally entered below the function mask.

- The variables field (*var*) allows supplementary variables to be given that reflect the results of the specified function.

Figure 6.3 demonstrates some of the concepts. Probably the most important consideration to be recognized is the fact that visual operations in the manual mode are represented lexically in the run mode. For example, the entry 12–3, denoting a starting column of 12 for three positions, is a data field in the function mask, and the entry 111 is the search key placed directly below it.

Another important consideration is that the run control statement format is divided into several sections, separated by spaces, and each of these sections includes positional parameters separated by commas. There are default assumptions that apply when a parameter is omitted, and also conventions that apply when a list is terminated. These assumptions and conventions are presented only when necessary to introduce an important concept.

Octal Type Algorithms

The mapping between MAPPER types and system data files is through an octal number, computed by way of a method that partitions the set of file numbers into groups of eight, the number of types in a mode. For example, type B in mode 16 has the octal number 202. There are two similar algorithms for computing it:

Method One (Octal arithmetic)
$(Even Mode_8 * 10_8) + Type_8$
Example: Type E in mode 40 is:
$(50_8 * 10_8) + 10_8 = 500_8 + 10 = 510_8$
Example: Type B in mode 16 is:
$(20 * 10_8) + 2_8 = 200_8 + 2_8 = 202_8$
Method Two (Decimal arithmetic)
$(Even Mode_{10} * 8_{10}) + Type_{10}$ and Convert to Octal
Example: Type E in mode 40 is:
$(40 * 8) + 8 = 328_{10} = 510_8$
Example: Type B in mode 16 is:
$(16 * 8) + 2 = 128 + 2 = 130_{10} = 202_8$

where the following type table is used:

Alpha Type	Octal Number	Decimal Number
A	–	–
B	2	2
C	4	4
D	6	6
E	10	8
F	12	10

Alpha Type	Octal Number	Decimal Number
G	14	12
H	16	14
I	20	16

Thus in the preceding statement:

$$@SRH,16,202,2 \ldots$$

the number 202 refers to type B in mode 16. As mentioned previously, it is likely that this "not so user-friendly" convention will be changed in the future.

There are two runs available to the end-user in the MAPPER system to help with the mode/type conversion: OTA performs octal to alpha conversion, and ATO performs alpha to octal conversion.

Variables and Reserved Words

In mathematics, a *variable* refers to an unknown quantity, and in some cases, to situations where a specific value does not matter to the concept being presented. It is necessary in many instances to develop an algorithm or procedure independently of specific values that would be determined during the course of events.

In the computer field, the word *variable* is often contrasted to a constant. Whereas the value of a constant is fixed, a variable can assume a set of values. Thus, the value of a variable is not constant, but subject to change.

In the MAPPER system, all variables begin with the letter V followed by a number that may be 1 through 199. For example, V8, V37, and V170 are valid variable names. The letter V denotes a variable, and the number makes it unique. A variable must be defined and it must be given a value.

A variable is defined when it is used for the first time. When a variable name first appears in a run control statement, it must also denote a data type (not to be confused with mode type) and specify an initial value. The following data types for variables are permitted in the MAPPER system:

Type	Designation	Size	Note
Alphanumeric	A	12	Arithmetic permitted
Alphanumeric	H	12	Arithmetic not permitted

Type	Designation	Size	Note
Integer	I	12	Whole numbers only
Numeric fractional	F	12	Numbers with fractions and decimal point
String	S	132	Character string data
Octal	O	12	Octal integers only

Accordingly, the following are valid variable definitions:

Variable	Note
V6I2	Integer variable with two places
V10A6	Alphanumeric variable with six places
V113F12	Fractional variable with 12 places
V76S20	String variable with 20 places

Variables are defined and assigned values in the various run control statements. The Search statement, given previously as:

@SRH,16,202,2 D 12-3 [,111 V1I3,V2I3

contains two variable definitions: V1 and V2. Both are integer variables with three places. As a result of the search operation, the MAPPER system places the number of matches into V1 and the number of lines searched into V2. Arithmetic can be performed on variables, as in:

@CHG V1 V1+1 .

which adds 1 to the value of V1. In statements involving variables and operators, spaces must be placed after all elements of the statement. A variable may be defined and assigned a value at the same time, as in:

@LDV V84H8=MAPPER .

which places the characters "MAPPER" into the variable named V8. There are a variety of ways to define variables and assign values in the MAPPER system. Each method has limitations and efficiency considerations. The Change (CHG) and Line Variable (LDV) statements are two of these options.

A reserved word is a name taken over by the MAPPER system. After the execution of certain MAPPER run control statements, status and informational indicators are set. There are two status indicators in the MAPPER system, STAT1 and STAT2; and a long list of informational indicators, such as RID$, TIME$, DATE1$, and TYPE$. The Binary

Fund run control statement, for example, returns a status code in STAT1 giving the result status of the operation. Similarly, the Add Report run control statement returns the new RID number in RID$. STAT1, STAT2, RID$, and so forth are reserved words. The following example of successive run control statements gives some indication of how variables and reserved words can be used:

```
@DUP,20,250,4 . DUPLICATE REPORT (XR MANUALLY)
@CHG V7I3 RID$ . PLACE NEW RID NUMBER IN V7
@DSP,20,250,V7 . DISPLAY IT
```

This example simply duplicates a report, and the new RID number is placed into the reserved word named RID$, which is stored in the variable named V7 in the second statement. The third statement displays the RID whose RID number is stored in variable V7.

Temporary RIDs

Each active MAPPER terminal possesses a unique operational domain, including work areas for temporary results. In the manual mode, one result area exists. When it is necessary to reference the result area, a minus (–) RID number is used.

In the run mode, the operational domain is more complex, and five temporary RIDs can be used. The primary result area is labeled –0, i.e. "minus zero," and the other four temporary RIDs are labeled –1 through –4. The following sample run gives an idea of how they may be used:

```
@SRH,20,250,4 ``10-4 [,1673 . RESULT IN RID -0
@DSP,20,250,-0 . DISPLAY RESULT IN -0
@RNM,20,250,-0 -1 . SAVE RID AS -1
@SOR,20,250,5 21-4,34-3 [,1,2D . REPLACE -0
@DSP,20,250,-0 . DISPLAY SECOND RESULT
@MCH,20,250,-0,20,250,-1 M 16-4,39-3 [,1,A 27-4,\
      52-3 [,1,A .
```

The example, which is essentially meaningless, uses RIDs –0 and –1, and demonstrates the Rename Function (RNM), which establishes a new reference for a RID. The backslash symbol (\) specifies a line continuation.

Utility Runs

The Octal-to-Alpha (OTA) runs, mentioned previously, are examples of utility runs that make it easier for the run design specialist to prepare runs. It might have crossed a person's mind by now as to how exactly in a run control statement, such as:

@SRH,20,250,4 ` `10-4 [,1673 .

a person actually obtains the field/character specification of 10-4 without counting columns. Moreover, counting columns, even if it is a feasible method, requires a copy of a report; and many MAPPER people prefer to work online, even to the extent that the HELP facility commonly replaces the MAPPER reference manual.

Three utility runs assist in the process of writing run control statements:

- The CC run gives a horizontal column count for a specified form type.

- The FCC run displays the field headers, the column position of the first character in each field, and the size of each field.

- The FORM run displays a definition of fields and subfields that constitute various run control statements.

Examples of runs CC, FCC, and FORM are given in Figures 6.4(a), 6.4(b), and 6.4(c), respectively. The value of these runs is evident from the information they provide.

```
          111111111122222222223333333333344444444445
 12345678901234567890123456789012345678901234567890
*ORD. DATE .CUS. CUSTOMER NAME .ST.AMOUNT.
*NUM.       .NUM.                  .  .    .
*===.======.===.================.==.======.
 687 830115 528                       12630
 688 830122 320                      471146
 689 830209 733                       86546
 690 830228 633                      101094
 691 830315 320                      233405
 692 830320 528                       61500
 693 830322 320                        2160
                  ..... END REPORT .....
```

(a) Example of the CC run.

```
.DATE 29 MAR 83   12:22:58     REPORT GENERATION     KATZAN
. MODE 270, TYPE 4162, RID 48,     ALPHA TYPE B     80 CHARACTER LINE LENGTH
*ORD. DATE .CUS. CUSTOMER NAME .ST.AMOUNT.
*NUM.      .NUM.                 .  .      .
*===.======.===.================.==.======.
 2-3 6-6    13-3                 33-2
                 17-15               36-6
```

```
..... END REPORT .....
```

(b) Example of the FCC run.

```
.DATE 29 MAR 83  12:31:08  RID      2   29 MAR 83  KATZAN
. SAMPLE MAPPER RUN                             BY:           I004200
*=====================
@SRH
@MCH
@TOT
@DSP
```

```
..... END REPORT .....
```

```
.DATE 29 MAR 83  12:25:07  RID      3   29 MAR 83  KATZAN
. SAMPLE MAPPER RUN                             BY:           I004200
*=====================
@SRH,MD,TP,RD,LINE,LINEQ,LABEL OPT CHR LNTP,PRM VNFNDS,VNLNS .
@MCH,MD1,TP1,RD1,MD2,TP2,RD2,LABEL OPT CHR LNTP,PRM CHR LNTP,PRM .
@TOT,MD,TP,RD,LABEL OPT CHR LNTP,PRM VNDATA .
@DSP,MD,TP,RD,LINE,TABQ,FMT,INTRM(Y/N),SH,MSG .
```

```
..... END REPORT .....
```

(c) Example of the FORM run.

Figure 6.4 Sample output from the CC, FCC, and FORM runs.

Run Design

The design of a MAPPER run is the straightforward process of mapping between manual functions and run control statements. In fact, it is suggested that run designers "think manual" in doing their work. At first, this might appear to be an unnecessary crutch. It turns out to be a practical necessity, however, because of the visual orientation of the MAPPER system.

This section gives a brief practical example of a MAPPER run and shows how the statements are mapped into manual functions. The *Order List* and *Customer List* reports, originally used as examples in Figure 4.10 are used here. The two reports are listed in Figures 6.5(a) and 6.5(b), followed by a listing of the run in Figure 6.5(c), and the result in Figure 6.5(d).

```
.DATE 23 MAR 83  10:19:34  RID     48    23 MAR 83
.                 ORDER LIST
*ORD. DATE .CUS. CUSTOMER NAME .ST.AMOUNT.
*NUM.       .NUM.                .  .      .
*===.======.===.================.==.======.
 687 830115 528                      12630
 688 830122 320                     471146
 689 830209 733                      86546
 690 830228 633                     101094
 691 830315 320                     233405
 692 830320 528                      61500
 693 830322 320                       2160
                   ..... END REPORT .....
```

(a) Receiving report used for search operation.

```
.DATE 23 MAR 83  10:27:55  RID     49    23 MAR 83
.        CUSTOMER LIST
*CUS. CUSTOMER NAME .ST.
*NUM.                .  .
*===.================.==.
 320 ACE ALUMINUM    NY
 528 GOOD STEEL      PA
 633 ALPHA MFG       CA
 733 FASTENERS INC   NC
                   ..... END REPORT .....
```

(b) Sending report.

```
.DATE 29 MAR 83  13:17:40  RID     2    29 MAR 83  KATZAN
. SAMPLE MAPPER RUN                               BY:           I004200
*====================
@SRH,270,4162,48 ' ' 13-3  ,320 .
@MCH,270,4162,49,270,4162,-0 M 2-3,6-15,22-2  ,1,A,B 13-3,17-15,33-2  ,1,A,B .
@TOT,270,4162,-0 ' ' 36-6  ,+ .
@DSP,270,4162,-0 .




                ..... END REPORT .....
```

(c) RID of run control lines.

```
.
.      3 LINES FOUND OUT OF 7 LINES
.
*            ***
*            320
.   .   .
.DATE 23 MAR 83  10:19:34  RID    48    23 MAR 83
.                 ORDER LIST
*ORD. DATE .CUS. CUSTOMER NAME .ST.AMOUNT.
*NUM.      .NUM.                .  .       .
*===.======.===.================.==.======.
 688 830122 320 ACE ALUMINUM    NY 471146
 691 830315 320 ACE ALUMINUM    NY 233405
 693 830322 320 ACE ALUMINUM    NY   2160

.GRAND-TOTAL  -
. AMOUNT       =    706711
                   ..... END REPORT .....
```

(d) Result.

Figure 6.5 Example of a run.

The run procedure is listed as follows:

- Select all lines from the *Order List* with Customer Numbers (CUS NUM) of 320.
- Match the result against the *Customer List* and extract and move the CUSTOMER NAME and state (ST) fields to the *Order List* report.
- Totalize the AMOUNT field.
- Display the result.

Mappings of the Search, Match, and Totalize run control statements with Search, Match, and Totalize function masks are given in Figures 6.6, 6.7, and 6.8, respectively.

Select all lines from the Order List with
Customer Numbers (CUS NUM) of 320

(a) Summary of the data processing operation.

@SRH,270,4162,48 ` `13-3 [,320.

(b) Statement.

```
.          ORDER LIST
*ORD. DATE .CUS. CUSTOMER NAME .ST.AMOUNT.
*NUM.          .NUM.              .  .        .
*===.======.===.================.==.======.
 *** ****** *** **************** ** ******
              320
```

(c) Mapping of the Search run control statement into a Search
function mask.

Figure 6.6 Example of a Search run control statement.

___

Match the result against the Customer List
and extract and move the CUSTOMER NAME and
state (ST) fields to the Order List report

(a) Summary of the data processing operation.

@MCH,270,4162,49,270,4162,–0 M 2–3,6–15,22–2\
[,1,A,B 13–3,17–15,33–2 [,1,A,B

(b) Statement.

```
.      CUSTOMER LIST
*CUS. CUSTOMER NAME .ST.
*NUM.                .  .
*===.================.==.
 *** **************** **
  1   A                B
.              ORDER LIST
*ORD. DATE .CUS. CUSTOMER NAME .ST.AMOUNT.
*NUM.          .NUM.              .  .        .
*===.======.===.================.==.======.
 *** ****** *** **************** ** ******
          1   A              B
```

(c) Mapping of the Match run control statement into a Match
function mask.

Figure 6.7 Example of a Match run control statement.

___

Totalize the AMOUNT field

(a) Summary of the data processing operation.

@TOT,270,4162,–0 ´ ´36–6 [,+.

(b) Statement.

```
    .            ORDER LIST
*ORD. DATE .CUS. CUSTOMER NAME .ST.AMOUNT.
*NUM.      .NUM.                . .       .
*===. ======. ===. ===============. ==. ======.
                                +
```

(c) Mapping of the Totalize run control statement into a Totalize function mask.

Figure 6.8 Example of a Totalize run control statement.

Run Control Statements

Several run control statements are widely used and also give a flavor for the MAPPER run structure. Ten statements are covered:

Control Word	Function
ADR	Add Report
DUP	Duplicate Report
DLR	Delete Report
REP	Replace Report
DSP	Display Report
RNM	Rename Report
SOR	Sort Report
SRH	Search Report
TOT	Totalize
MCH	Match Reports

The format for each statement is given along with a single example. Whenever possible, the following abbreviations (see Figure 6.2) are used:

Abbreviation	Meaning
m	Mode
t	Type
r	RID
opt	Options
pos	Column and field character positions
line	Line type
prm	Parameter specifications
var	Variables

The *Add Report* statement adds a new report to a specified report type, and places the new RID number into RID$. It has the following form:

@ADR,m,t .

The following statement adds a report to mode 20 type E:

@ADR,20,250 .
@CHG V9l3 RID$.

(The CHG statement places the new RID number into variable V9.)

The *Duplicate Report* statement duplicates an existing report in the same mode and type, and places the new RID number into RID$. It has the following form:

@DUP,m,t,r .

The following statement duplicates RID 3E in mode 20:

@DUP,20,250,3 .
@CHG V10l3 RID$

(Similar to the above case, the CHG statement places the new RID number to variable V10.)

The *Delete Report* statement deletes a report from the MAPPER system. Manually, only the last person to update a report can delete it, but this restriction is ignored in the run mode. The statement has the following form:

@DLR,m,t,r .

The following statement deletes RID 5E in mode 20:

@DLR,20,250,5 .

The *Replace Report* statement replaces a receiving report with a sending report, ignoring update security procedures. The form of the statement is:

@REP,m ,t ,r ,m ,t ,r

(where replacement goes from subscript 1 to subscript 2).

The following statement replaces RID 9E with RID3E:

@REP,20,250,3,20,250,9 .

If the sending report is the result RID (-0), then it need not be specified, as in:

@REP,20,250,15 .

which replaces RID 15E with the contents of –0.

The *Display Report* statement displays a report on the user's terminal, and has the form:

@DSP,m,t,r,*start-line,tab,format,interim*

where:

- *start-line* gives the line number in the report to start the display.

- *tab* is the tab position to place the cursor after the report has been displayed.

- *format* is the report format.

- *interim* means that the display is interim—denoted by Y— and that the run need not be resumed with the resume (RSM) key.

The following statement displays report 2E:

@DSP,20,250,2 .

In this case, line 1, format 1, and no resume are assumed, and a default tab position is used. The following statements perform a search and a display:

@SRH,20,250,3,5 DH 37-6 [,MAPPER .
@DSP,20,250,-0 .

The Display Report statement should be placed alone on a control line because of the operational properties of MAPPER.

The *Rename* statement works in conjunction with temporary RIDs named –1, –2, –3, and –4. Through the Rename statement, a new temporary reference is made to existing reports. The simple form of the Rename command is:

@RNM -n

which renames the result area –0. The following example renames area –0 to –4:

@RNM -4

A second form of the Rename statement allows a stored RID—called a positive RID—to be temporarily renamed to serve as a "working copy:"

@RNM,m,t,r -n

The following statement assigns RID 9E to temporary RID –2:

@RNM,20,250,9 –2 .

The *Sort* statement sorts the data in a report by one or more key fields by ascending, descending, or numeric order. The form of the Sort statement is:

@SOR,m,t,r opt pos line,prm

The following statement sorts RID 3E by columns 37 through 6 in descending order:

@SOR,20,250,3 ' '37–6 [,1D .

and the following statement sorts the previous result by columns 2 through 7 in ascending order and columns 23 through 2 in descending order:

@SOR,20,250,–0 ' '2–7,23–2 [,1,2D .

The *Search Report* statement scans a report for specified conditions and produces a report result. It has the following form:

@SRH,m,t,r,*start-line,num-lines,label*
opt pos line,prm var

where:

- *start-line* is the line number to start the search.
- *num-lines* is the number of lines to search.
- *label* is the statement number to go to if there are no successes.

The following statement searches for all occurrences of "CA" in columns 74 through 2 in RID 9E:

@SRH,20,250,9 DH 74–2 [,CA .

This case demonstrates that unused parameters at the end of a positional parameter field can be deleted. The following statement searches for all occurrences of "CA" and "94310" in the same RID:

@SRH,20,250,9 DH 74–2,77–5 [,CA,94310 .

The following statement searches for all occurrences of (CA and 94310) or (NY and 10014) in the same RID:

@SRH,20,250,9 DH 74–2,77–5 [,CA,94310/[,NY,10014 .

The slash (/) character means "go to the next line in the function mask." The final example searches for all dates in the range of 1979 to 1983 in the same RID:

@SRH,20,250,9 DH 13-4 [,1979/R,1983 .

where "R" in this case denotes the range specification that would be placed in the function mask.

The *Totalize* statement performs arithmetic and data movement on data fields in reports, and has the following form:

@TOT,m,t,r,*label* opt pos line,prm var

where *label* is the statement label to go to if there are no lines found. The following example totals the values in columns 23 through 2 of RID 3E, and displays the result:

@TOT,20,250,3 ' '23-2 [,+ .
@DSP,20,250,-0 .

For the same RID, the following example takes the data values in columns 37 through 3, subtracts the data values in 47 through 2, and places the result in 54-4. Then column 54-4 is totaled and the result is displayed:

@TOT,20,250,3 ' '23-2,37-3,47-2,54-4\
[,+,+,-,=/[,,,,+ .

In the latter case, commas are required to effectively "skip over" columns that are not used in the second line of the function mask.

The *Match* statement is used to match fields in two reports and perform data movement from a sending to a receiving report, as specified. The form of the statement is:

@MCH,m_1,t_1,r_1,m_2,t_2,r_2, *label* opt pos_1 $line_1$, prm_1
pos_2 $line_2$,prm_2

where subscript 1 denotes the sending report, subscript 2 denotes the receiving report, and *label* is the statement number to go to if no matches are found. The following example transfers the contents of positions 41 through 8 from the sending report 2E to positions 13 through 8 of the receiving report 9E. The fields to be matched are 21-2 in the sending report and 37-2 in the receiving report.

@MCH,20,250,2,20,250,9,10 P 21-2,41-8\
[,1,A 13-8,37-2 [,A,1 .

The P option denotes presorted fields. The Match function, both manually and under run control, will work with unsorted fields, but presorted fields are preferable because of efficiency considerations.

Summary

A *run* is a set of run control statements that gives the step-by-step procedure for performing a specific set of data processing operations or a report generation. A run control statement is essentially a MAPPER command, along with its parameters, specified in a free form line. All manual commands have counterparts as run control statements. In addition, the run facility in MAPPER contains statements that deal with the automatic mode of operation, such as the capability for performing conditional logic and input/output. The run control statements composing a run are stored as free form lines in a RID; the RID is assigned a name that is registered with the MAPPER coordinator, so that security and various authorization conventions can be maintained. A run is executed by entering its name in the control line and transmitting it to the computer. A run is executed by the MAPPER run control facility by successively selecting statements, interpreting them, and then executing them.

Run control statements have a fixed format that is consistently applied, so that standard terminology and operational conventions apply to it. Each statement begins with the "at" symbol (@), followed by a control word that gives the command to be executed. Some typical control words are @DSP... for Display and @TOT... for Totalize. More than one run control statement may be placed on a single line; the last statement on a line should be terminated with a period (.). Comments may follow the period.

The run control statement format contains several fields, each containing several parameters separated by commas. This concept is demonstrated by the following examples:

```
@SRH,20,250,2 D 12-3 [,111 V1I3,V2I3 .
@TOT,20,250,3 ` `23-2,37-3,47-2,54-4 [,+,+,-,=/\
     [,,,,+ .
@MCH,20,250,2,20,250,9,10 P 21-2,41-8 [,1,A 13-8\
     37-2 [,A,1 .
```

The most important consideration to be recognized is the fact that visual operations in the manual mode are represented lexically in the run mode.

The mapping between MAPPER types and system data files is through an octal number, computed by ways of a method that partitions the set of file numbers into groups of eight, the number of types in a mode. For example, type B in mode 16 has the octal number 202. Algorithms and special runs are available for conversion between the alphabetic and octal notations.

In the MAPPER system, all variables begin with the letter V followed by a number that may be 1 through 199. V8, V37, and V170, for example, are valid variable names. The letter V denotes a variable, and it must be given a value. A variable is defined and assigned a value the first time it appears in a run control statement, and it must contain a type specification. MAPPER variables may be alphanumeric, integer, fractional, string, and octal.

A reserved word is a name taken over by the MAPPER system. After the execution of certain MAPPER run control statements, status and informational indicators are set. There are two status indicators, STAT1 and STAT2; and a long list of informational indicators, such as RID$, TIME$, DATE1$, and TYPE$.

Each active MAPPER terminal possesses a unique operational domain, including work areas for temporary results. In the manual mode, one result area exists. When it is necessary to reference the result area, a minus (-) RID number is used.

In the run mode, the operational domain is more complex, and five temporary RIDs can be used. The primary result area is labeled –0, i.e. "minus zero," and the other four temporary RIDs are labeled –1 through –4.

Utility runs assist in making the process of writing run control statements. The utility runs are particularly useful for run design:

- The CC run gives a horizontal column count for a specified form type.
- The FCC run displays the field headers, the column position of the first character in each field, and the size of each field.
- The FORM run displays a definition of fields and subfields that constitute various run control statements.

The design of a MAPPER run is the straightforward process of mapping between manual functions and run control statements. In fact, it is suggested that run designers "think manual" in doing their work. At first, this might appear to be an unnecessary crutch. It turns out to be a practical necessity, however, because of the visual orientation of the MAPPER system.

Several run control statements are widely used and also give a flavor for the MAPPER structure. Ten varied statements serve this purpose:

Control Word	Function
ADR	Add report
DUP	Duplicate report
DLR	Delete report
REP	Replace report
DSP	Display report
RNM	Rename report
SOR	Sort report
SRH	Search report
TOT	Totalize
MCH	Match reports

While the MAPPER system contains a high number of manual functions and run control statements, the run concept allows the user to extend the system to satisfy the needs of a particular operational domain.

CHAPTER SEVEN

Organizational Dynamics

The MAPPER system is more than a system or a language, or even a combination of the two. It is a unique means of doing data processing, report generation, data entry, database management, information management, computer graphics, and even office automation. In being all of these things, the MAPPER system can impact the data processing department and the end-user group in several ways, ranging from organizational structure to operational dynamics. It can effect how their computing needs are satisfied, and can determine the people who actually participate in the informational activities of the organization.

Application Domain

The interlocking facilities that constitute the MAPPER system effectively determine its application domain. The interactive online facilities of the MAPPER system that provide real time response to user requests make the system particularly appropriate for the following activities:

- Ad hoc reporting.
- Frequent updating of data.
- Data entry.
- Database applications.
- End-user involvement in application development.

- Traditional data processing operations with a limited scope.

The system does not lend itself in general to high volume data processing and reporting operations, commonly associated with batch processing. However, the end-user can apply a wide range of traditional data processing operations, such as searching and sorting, to data stored in the MAPPER database.

Once a report form is established in the MAPPER system, routine reporting, updating, data entry, database processing, and other data processing operations can be conveniently performed by persons with a minimal knowledge of computer and data processing technology. Some of the most frequently used functions in this category are:

- Data entry and modification.
- Line-oriented access and modification operations.
- Report-oriented inquiry and update operations.
- Query operations for specific data.
- Calculation facilities.
- Display and printing operations.

To sum up, data can be changed, added, deleted, moved around, totaled and summarized, selected, projected, and finally displayed or printed. Clearly, these functions can be performed with other software tools. With MAPPER, all of this can be done in real-time and interactively through a host-based facility that gives the advantage of economy-of-scale to end-user computing requirements.

The MAPPER system also has connectivity to system software and access to system data files through well-defined data interfaces. Thus, data can be extracted and summarized from existing databases with utility programs and special software, and transferred to the MAPPER system for manipulation and reporting, as covered above. The MAPPER system can co-exist with other applications or run as a standalone system.

A key advantage of the MAPPER system is that the end-user has direct control over data storage, data processing, and data reporting—all through a single software interface, which is the MAPPER system. MAPPER file structures are standard across the system, and conventional software debugging is not necessary. Moreover, the software maintenance problem of adapting to rapid changes in requirements does not exist in the MAPPER system because of its interactive modality and its high level of end-user involvement. Because of the short lead time to get a MAPPER application going, the system can be applied to requirements with a short time span, and can be used to develop application prototypes prior to conventional applications software development.

The MAPPER system is data communications based. This characteristic effectively determines that end-users, be they programmers, analysts, or application specialists, can communicate with each other through the resources of the host and communications facilities of the system. Through specially prepared runs, the MAPPER system can be used in an office environment for the following activities:

- Word processing capability for managers and professionals.
- Day-to-day calendars.
- Day-to-day reminders.
- Phone/visit logs.
- Electronic mail.
- Distribution lists.
- Departmental activity logs.
- Scheduling of meetings.
- Scheduling of facilities.
- Historical calendars.
- Calculator facilities.
- Financial calculations.
- Telephone directory.
- Suspense filing.
- Affinity support.
- Document creation and distribution.
- Electronic paper clip facilities.

The above list of activities clearly separates the application domain of the MAPPER system into two operational modes:

- Problem solving.
- Communications.

Any function that involves more than a trivial amount of processing and input/output time is generically classed as *problem solving*. Any function that requires only a minimal amount of processing and input/output time is classed as *communications*. Most office functions are communications-based, except for word processing, document creation, and financial calculations. Reporting functions would fall into the problem solving class.

Clearly, the potential capability of the MAPPER system is strong in both categories. Since almost all access to MAPPER is online, however, communications-based functions can be realized at minimal cost after the reporting system is installed.

The MAPPER Coordinator

The *MAPPER coordinator* is a person or a group of people who is responsible for the control of the MAPPER system and the manner in which it is used. More specifically, coordinator duties concern the design, implementation, control, and maintenance of the MAPPER reporting database, and the relationship between the reporting database and other system data files on the host computer. As a discipline, the coordinator position involves coordination between systems people and the present and future user group—hence the name "coordinator"—and incorporates the planning and policy making of traditional data processing. The essence of the coordinator position is management, i.e. mangement of the MAPPER system. The scope of the job may also include people management, as well.

As a concept, the MAPPER coordinator is both a control point and a function. As a control point, the coordinator position constitutes a central resource within the organization providing a structural link between the following units:

- User management.
- Data processing management.

- End users.
- Data processing personnel.
- Computer operations.

In some organizations, user management and end-users will be application specialists, such as bankers, accountants, or engineers. In other cases, systems and business analysts will assume a user role and provide an operational link between the data processing department and the true end-user of the system.

From a functional viewpoint, the coordinator provides *Global Balance* (GLOBALANCE) to the MAPPER system by performing tasks dealing with the following subjects:

- System and data integrity.
- System and data security.
- Performance analysis.
- Capacity planning.
- Anticipation of user requirements.
- Training.
- Consulting with current and prospective MAPPER users.
- Application design and development.
- Documentation of services.
- Scheduling of services.
- Database design.

A MAPPER system without GLOBALANCE can easily become an appendage to the data processing department without providing any of the productivity benefits normally associated with end-user computing.

In addition to a reasonably high number of ancillary tasks, the two primary functions of the MAPPER coordinator are registration and monitoring. *Registration* relates to the incorporation into the MAPPER system of new users, terminals, runs, and passwords. Associated with registration are the changes that occur during daily operation. *Monitoring* involves a reasonably careful ongoing analysis of resources used by various MAPPER applications against planned utilization, and a global assessment of operational statistics from input/output activity, log files, recovery files, and report update files.

To sum up, the MAPPER coordinator is responsible for the total operation of the system, from application design to the scheduling of MAPPER services. A key function of the coordinator is to work closely with computer operations personnel.

In small MAPPER systems, a single person can perform all coordinator functions, and perhaps can develop some applications, as well. In a medium to large-sized MAPPER shop, it is likely that there will be too much to do for a single person. In the latter case, the coordinator function can be staffed by a "coordinator team" or by a coordinator manager and several specialists dealing with complex topics, such as applications design and data communications.

Information Center Concept

The user environment for data processing and reporting is dynamic; this contention is strongly supported by the high level of maintenance costs in most data processing installations. Because of this fact and the growing applications backlog, an "information center" is commonly considered in the computer industry as a viable means of providing users access to data in their own environment with the end objective of making them self-sufficient from a data processing viewpoint.

An *information center* is a group within an enterprise formed to facilitate end-user participation in the following activities:

- Application program development.
- Access to enterprise databases.
- Data planning for the enterprise.
- Development of system prototypes.

The information center concept is an alternative to traditional application development, because it fosters end-user development rather than data processing development. In some instances, the Information Center (IC) will be organized within the data processing department, and its manager will report directly to the top data processing manager. In other cases, an Information Center will be established in a headquarters or central location to provide a high level of user assistance without being unduly encumbered by data processing policies and procedures. The Information Center staff for the most part will be people with computer experience and knowledge of how the enterprise operates.

The Information Center will provide services to the end-users that are not offered by the EDP/MIS department. As a group, the Information Center will select the appropriate end-user tools, manage data bases, and provide access to those data bases. Effectively, then, the objective of the Information Center is to supply the client population with productivity assistance that enhances access to the organization's informational resource and increases the self-sufficiency of the user in a computer environment.

The motivation for the formation of an Information Center is largely the result of both increased needs on the part of the user and a decrease in the capability of the EDP/MIS department to satisfy these and other needs. In short, there is a backlog of applications to be developed in most EDP/MIS shops, and an increase in requirements for services that are not satisfied by conventional transaction and report processing.

User support activities of an Information Center can be direct or indirect. Direct activities are user education, consulting, and direct assistance. The latter category necessarily includes a user help desk and a "hot line" for debugging assistance. *Consulting* is important for assisting the user in the selection of proper hardware and software tools, and to ensure that an end-user is heading in the right direction. *Education* is an ongoing activity to acquaint new users with Information Center services and to update older users to new developments. Indirect activities involve the management of computer and informational resources, and how the Information Center itself is managed. Continuous activities in this area include hardware and software evaluation, security, data base administration, technical development, planning, and other administrative and managerial tasks.

The Information Center concept is beneficial to the EDP/MIS department, even though it may not seem that way on the surface. With an Information Center, highly trained computer personnel are better utilized, while the effective service to the end-user community is improved. The application programming backlog is reduced as is the need for application program maintenance.

The Information Center organization can report to the top EDP/MIS managers or exist as an independent unit. When the Information Center organization does not, in fact, report to the EDP/MIS department, then careful planning is required to help ensure that activities are appropriate to the fostering group. The EDP/MIS department should have influence over the operation of the Information Center.

Analysis

At this point in time, the practice of end-user computing appears to be an objective rather than a reality. To be sure, end-users in companies like the Sperry Corporation and IBM do in fact engage in data processing and report preparation. Clearly, there are others, but they appear to be exceptions. The computer field is definitely heading in this direction, however, and it is likely that the swing to nonprocedural languages and end-user computing will gather momentum as time passes. Many end-users, who are not computer specialists, are currently using computers for business purposes, but they are employing "canned" solutions to structured problems.

The greatest benefit of nonprocedural and end-user systems is to the data processing department. The applications backlog can be reduced and a higher level of quality service can be provided to their customers. The primary objective of the data processing department is: "To manage data and get it to the end-user." This objective holds for data processing and office automation, as well.

Several MAPPER installations have adapted the information center concept to the needs of their organization, and also to the realities of application software development, by establishing an information center within the data processing department to assist their own people in preparing applications for the end-user community.

The name Solution Center is proposed for an information center providing MAPPER service within the data processing department. Clearly, that is what it is. There are several benefits to this arrangement:

- The intricacies of run design—one of the primary advantages of the MAPPER system—can easily be mastered by data processing personnel.
- Since MAPPER is basically a nonprocedural system, programming as it is generally known is not done. Thus, programmers can be upgraded to analysts and develop application specialties.

- The MAPPER coordinator can be drawn from the data processing department, and this position can provide excellent experience in organizational dynamics.

- Procedures and standards for utilization of the MAPPER system can be readily established.

Clearly, the challenge with the MAPPER system is application and database design, and the solution center concept strongly supports this direction on a global and local scale.

A constantly reccuring problem with end-user systems in particular and data processing in general is data administration. The end-user and the application specialist have a crucial need to know:

- What data is in the system.

- What the data represents.

- What is its structure.

- How is it accessed.

Accordingly, application and subject database design are major considerations.

References

Bryce, M. "Information Resource Mismanagement," *Infosystems* (2/83), pp. 88–92.

Hammond, L.W. "Management Considerations for an Information Center," *IBM Systems Journal*, Volume 21, Number 2 (1982), pp. 131–161.

Hofstadter, D.R. "Metamagical Themes," *Scientific American*, Volume 248, Number 1 (January, 1983), p. 14.

Kull, D. "Information Centers Help Users Put It All Together," *Computer Decisions* (February, 1983), pp. 70–76.

MacDonald, A. "Visual Programming," *Datamation* (January, 1983), pp. 132–140.

"Managing and Integrating Information: The Essence of Office Automation," *Infosystems*, Volume 29, Number 6, Part 2 (June, 1982), special issue, pp. 1–24.

O'Connell, D.J. "The Information Resource Center," *Computerworld Office Automation*, Volume 16, Number 39A (September 29, 1982), pp. 35–38.

Rhodes, W.L. Jr. "The Information Center Extends a Helping Hand," *Infosystems* (183), pp. 26–30.

Schlueter, Louis Jr. *User-Designed Computing*, Lexington, Massachusetts: Lexington Books, 1982.

Sperry Univac Series 1100 publications:
- MAPPER 1100 User Guide, Form UP-9193, 1982.
- MAPPER 1100 Coordinator Reference, Form UP-9194, 1982.
- MAPPER 1100 Operator Reference, Form UP-9195, 1980.

The Sperry Corporation, St. Paul, Minnesota, 55164.

Thierauf, R.J. *Decision Support Systems for Effective Planning and Control: A Case Study Approach*, Englewood Cliffs, New Jersey: Prentice-Hall, Inc., 1982.

Index

A

Abort function, 44
Access and modification
  functions, 39, 62
Active system logo, 34, 38
Add a line, 46, 63
Add on command (ADON), 57,
  63
Add report (AR), 26, 36, 54, 63
Add report statement (ADR),
  102, 119, 124
Add to command (ADTO), 59,
  63
Application development, 3
Applications backlog, 2, 17
Arithmetic, 111
Arithmetic function (A), 86, 98
Ascending sort, 76
Asterisk, 28
Asterisk line, 28, 30, 37
At sign (@), 102, 123
Auxiliary command (AUX), 61,
  63
Averaging option, 96, 100

B

Backslash symbol (\), 112
Benefits of end-user computing, 4
Binary find function (BF), 78,
  84

C

Calculator facility, 85
Change a password, 34
Change function, 83, 84
Change statement (CHG), 111
Coded password, 34
Column-formed line, 27–28, 30,
  37
Column heading, 29, 37
Column one, 27
Comment line, 28, 30
Concurrent database access, 2
Continuation character, 112
Control line, 30–33
Control point, 12, 19, 130
Coordinator, 11
Cumulative option, 98, 100
Cursor, 45
Customer list report, 115

D

Data line, 29, 37
Date line, 29, 37
Delete report (DR), 63
Delete report statement (DLR),
  119, 125
Deleting lines, 49, 63
Department number, 34, 38
Descending sort, 77
Display report (D), 41, 42

Display report statement (DSP), 119, 125

Duplicate report (XR), 26, 36, 56, 63

Duplicate report statement (DUP), 119, 125

E

80–20 rule, 9–10, 19
End report line, 30, 37
End-user
concept, 2
system, 17
Entry counting option, 98, 100
Escalation of requirements, 16
Even mode, 24, 36
Evolutionary systems, 10, 19
Experimental report, 26, 36

F

Fast access method, 44
Field changes, 45, 63
File
drawer, 23, 36
folder, 23, 36
Filing cabinet, 23, 36
Filling fields option, 98, 100
Find function (F), 69, 83
Format position (FMT), 32, 38
Formed report, 24
Free form line, 27–28, 37
Function keyword (FUN), 41, 62

G

Global balance, 131

H

Header line, 29, 37
Help keyword (HELP), 41, 42, 62
Hold characters keyword (HLD CHRS), 33, 38
Horizontal arithmetic option, 91, 100
Horizontal movement option, 90, 100

I

Idle logo, 33, 35, 38
Information center, 15, 20, 132
Information system, 8
Inquiry and update functions, 65
Insert mode, 49, 63

J

Join operation, 80

K

Knowledge workers, 5–6, 18

L

Label, 122
Line
changes, 45, 63
continuation, 112
hierarchy, 30
-oriented functions, 39, 45, 53, 62, 63
position (LINE), 32, 38
size, 26, 36

type, 27–28
Load variable statement (LDV), 111
Locate function (LOC), 73, 84

M

Maintaining, Preparing, and Producing Executive Reports, 21, 35
Management support, 6
Management support system, 7, 18
Manual filing system, 23, 36
MAPPER
    coordination job, 23
    coordinator, 130
    database structure, 23, 36
    logo, 33
    see also Maintaining, Preparing, and Producing Executive Reports
    system, 21
Match
    function (MA), 80, 84
    statement (MCH), 122, 125
    update function, 83, 84
Meme, 11
Message waiting key (MSG WAIT), 44
Mode, 23, 36
Mode change command (M), 42
Mode pair, 24
Model report, 26
Money report, 89, 91
Monitoring, 131
Move mode, 49
Moving lines, 51–52, 63

O

Octal type algorithms, 109, 124
Odd mode, 24, 36
Open access, 3
Operational
    environment, 5
    philosophy, 44
Order list report, 115
Order report, 92
Ownership, 7

P

Password, 34, 38
Period, 27, 28
Period line, 28
Personal business computers, 20
Print command (PRINT), 61, 63
Production workers, 5
Productivity, 4
Prototype report, 17

Q

Quick-and-dirty compromise, 16

R

Read only access, 24, 36
Read/write access, 24, 36
Registration, 131
Release function, 44
Rename statement (RNM), 120, 125
Repaint the screen command (PNT), 45–46, 63
Replace report (REP), 26, 36, 57, 63

Replace report statement (REP), 119, 124
Replicate a line, 47, 63
Report
    creation, 26
    definition, 25
    format, 26
    heading, 28
    identification, 24, 36
    in general, 23, 36
    -oriented functions, 39, 54, 62, 63
    processing system, 21
    structure, 29
Reserved word, 111, 124
Result report, 73, 83
Resume keyword (RSM), 69
RID, see Report Identification
Roll position (RL), 32, 38, 41
Rounding option, 98, 100
Run
    control facility, 102
    control line, 102
    control statement format, 107, 123
    design, 114, 124
RUN facility, 23, 35

S

Search
    function (S), 70, 83
    list function, 83, 84
    list update function, 83, 84
    report statement (SRH), 121, 125
    update function, 83, 84
Sequencing option, 98, 100
Service functions, 39, 40, 62
Shift position (SHFT), 32, 38

Shortage of programmers, 1
Sign
    off, 35, 38
    on, 33
    on procedure, 34, 38
Slash character (/), 122
Sort
    function (SORT), 66, 75, 84
    mask, 75
    statement (SOR), 121, 125
Spreadsheet-like calculations, 99
Start-of-entry character, 45
Station idle logo, 33, 35, 38
Subformat, 26, 37
Subtotaling option, 95, 100
Support people, 5, 18
Systems and languages, 3

T

Tab set line, 28, 37
Temporary RID, 112, 124
Terminal period character (.), 102, 123
Think manual, 104, 125
Title line, 29, 37
Totalize
    function (TOT), 88, 99
    statement (TOT), 122, 125
Trailer line, 30
Transaction-oriented people, 5
Type, 23, 36
Type characteristics, 27
Type command (T), 41
Typical MAPPER functions, 22

U

Unplanned aspect, 3
User friendly, 62

User identification, 34, 38
Utility run, 113, 124

Variable, 110, 124
Vertical summation option, 93,
  100
Visual operation, 45
Visual programming, 21, 35, 65,
  83